I0828309

PAST & PRESENT

# PLANO

**Opposite:** A farmer and his son are seen "breaking stubble" (plowing the field after harvest to promote composting) with a double-disk plow in 1926 or 1927. Pictured are E.W. Stewart working the Rasor Farm with mules Kit and Coley and a pony named Nell. (Courtesy of the Plano Public Library.)

Past & Present

# PLANO

Mary Jacobs, Cheryl Smith, and Jeff Campbell
with photographs by Jennifer Shertzer

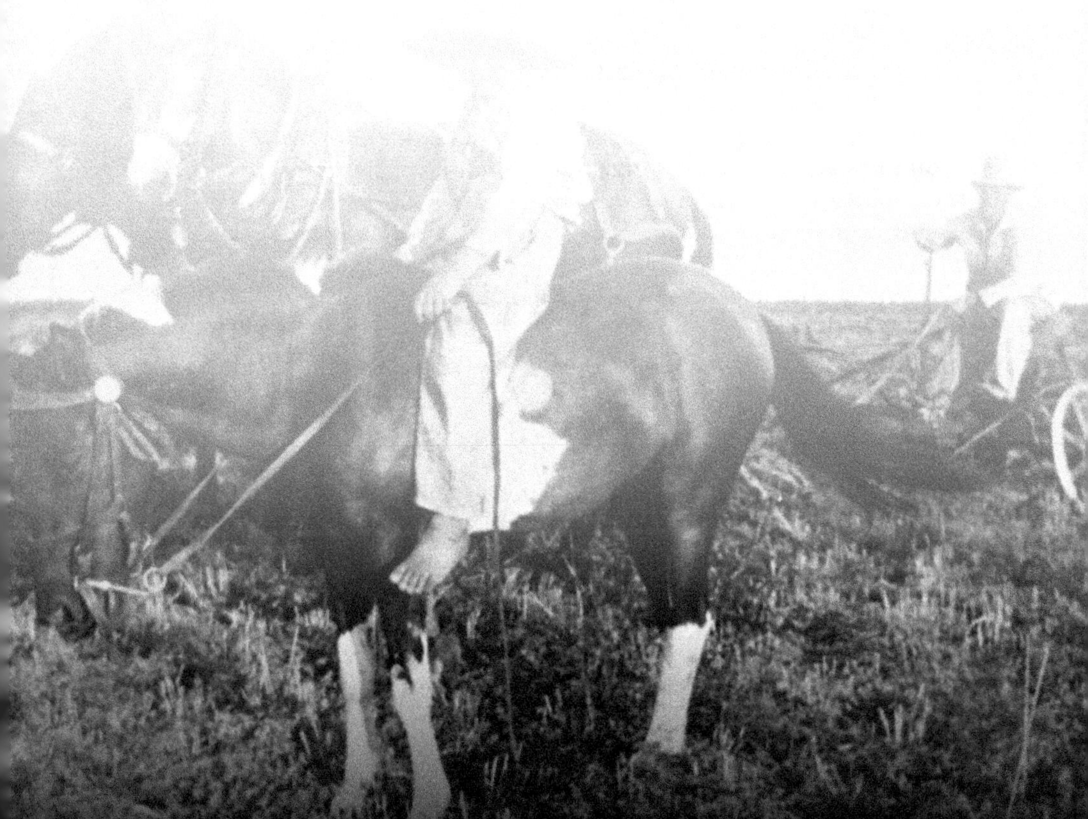

*In memory of Sid Wall, one of the founders of the Plano Conservancy for Historic Preservation, who passed away in 2023.*



ISBN 9781540257574

Library of Congress Control Number: 2023939491

Published by Arcadia Publishing
Charleston, South Carolina

For all general information, please contact Arcadia Publishing:
Telephone 843-853-2070
Fax 843-853-0044
E-mail sales@arcadiapublishing.com
For customer service and orders:
Toll-Free 1-888-313-2665

Visit us on the Internet at www.arcadiapublishing.com

**On the Front Cover:** Views of downtown Plano, looking east on 15th Street, taken during the great fire of 1895 and in 2023. (Courtesy of the Plano Public Library and Jennifer Shertzer.)

**On the Back Cover:** The home of Olney Davis, one of Plano's early prominent citizens. (Courtesy of the Plano Public Library.)

# Contents

# Acknowledgments

All "past" photographs in the book, except where noted, are courtesy of Plano Public Library. Genealogy librarian Cheryl Smith assembled the photographs from Collin County Images, the library's collection of photographs, documents, yearbooks, and other archive material representing the people and places of Collin County. Collin County Images is online, with the original material housed at the Genealogy Center at Haggard Library. All "present" photographs, except where noted, were taken by photographer Jennifer Shertzer. The captions and other text were written by writer Mary Jacobs. Jeff Campbell sourced the images from the Interurban Railway Museum.

The authors wish to thank the people who contributed photographs, and many are named throughout the book. The authors are also grateful for the many Plano residents and former residents who dug through their own files, located images, arranged photo shoots, or provided other assistance. Our long, but probably incomplete, list includes City of Plano staffers Mary Wright, Cindy Pierce, Dee Dee Falls, and Jason Fehrm; City of Plano's Parks and Recreation Department staff members Pam Holland, Ken Sumrow, Krisztina Kovacs, and Susie Hergenrader; retired city staff members Frank Turner and Don Wendell; Wendi Douglas and Jennifer Chapman with the Plano Police Department; Daniel Daly with Plano Fire-Rescue; Debbie Calvin of the Johnnie J. Myers Transportation Research Center; Jessica Kaszynski and Catherine Riggle at Children's Health; Mollie Hancock and Cody Baker of Ebby Halliday Realtors; Roy Wilshire; Kemper Smith; Steve Lavine; Luke Shertzer; Clint Haggard; Rodney Haggard; Randy Wright; Dollie Thomas; and Gwen Workman.

Dozens of volunteers posed in the modern photographs. Many are identified in the captions; those "models" not identified elsewhere include Brett Cooper, Michael Klein, Len Fossier, Bennett Ratliff, Clinton Bales, Karen Bellessa, James Gilbreath, Giselle Gazda, and Young Jenkins.

Special thanks go to John Brooks and members of the Plano History (& Nostalgia) Facebook group; John provided extensive help in pinpointing the locations of landmarks that are no longer in existence. The authors also wish to thank Jason Lavine for deploying his drone on a Sunday afternoon to create the modern versions of two vintage aerial photographs exclusively for this book.

# Introduction

What brought you to Plano? Some "Planoites" have lived here all their lives. Many arrived more recently, in the 1990s or later. Many were drawn to Plano's long list of amenities and advantages: excellent schools, outstanding parks, and extraordinary police, fire, and EMS services that make Plano one of the safest cities of its size in the nation. And many came for opportunity: the opportunity of a job, starting a business, or obtaining a good education.

Opportunity brought Plano's first Anglo residents to Plano, and today, opportunity continues to bring people from around the world to Plano.

In the early 1840s, the opportunity was land. The Republic of Texas offered free land to white men—640 acres for a married man and 320 for a single man—who cultivated the land for three years. The area that is now Plano was particularly attractive, boasting the best and richest blackland in North Texas and possibly the United States.

Life was hard on the frontier, but a community soon emerged. By 1850, the Plano area had its first school, its first cemetery, and a Methodist class, the beginnings of what today is First United Methodist Church of Plano. Small communities, with names like Lebanon and Bethany, dotted the area with their own schools and churches. Back then, the area that is now Plano was too big to traverse to get to church or school.

In 1864, Andy Drake, a formerly enslaved man, became the first Black person to settle in Plano. Together with Mose Stimpson, Drake founded the historically Black Douglass community in the 1860s, named after abolitionist Frederick Douglass. Many of Drake's and Stimpson's descendants still reside in Douglass today.

Life changed dramatically in Plano with the arrival of the railroad. In 1872, the Houston & Texas Central Railway connected downtown to an 872-mile line that eventually stretched from Houston northward to Dallas and Denison, with branches to Austin and Waco. Later, the St. Louis Southwestern Railway, popularly known as the "Cotton Belt," linked Plano to its line from St. Louis, Missouri, to various points in Arkansas, Tennessee, Louisiana, and Texas. Downtown Plano became the prosperous center of a booming farm economy, thanks to the emergence of cotton as a cash crop, cheap fencing, and mechanized farm equipment.

The city was incorporated in 1873. City leaders established Plano's school system, with the first high school class graduating in 1892. The mayor's office, city council, and city court were also established in 1881, initially meeting in the back of a saddlery shop. During this pivotal period, Plano also faced many challenges. Fires plagued the downtown area, destroying multiple buildings downtown in 1881, 1889, 1895, and again in 1897.

In the first half of the 20th century, Plano emerged as a small but forward-looking town. The city established a modern infrastructure—electricity and telephone service, trash collection, and a sewer system, as well as parcel post and door-to-door mail service. In 1925, Plano became one of the first towns of its size in Texas with paved streets. The Interurban Railway opened in 1908, linking Plano to Denison and Dallas.

Plano's years as a farming-based economy concluded around 1950 with the arrival of small industry and the growing interest of developers. Probably the single most important factor contributing to Plano's growth was the extension of the North Central Expressway from Campbell Road to Plano in 1957.

As automobiles became widely available and affordable, Plano was again transformed, this time as a suburb. The city became an attractive option for people who worked in Dallas but wanted to live in a more residential area. By 1960, Plano was the fastest-growing city in Collin County. New subdivisions began to crop up like mushrooms; schools and libraries were added to serve the growing population.

In 1979, Electronic Data Systems (EDS) purchased nearly 2,000 acres of land, with plans to relocate its corporate headquarters to west Plano. In the last 20 years, Plano transformed once again, from a bedroom community to a large city, becoming home to headquarters or regional operations of major corporations like Toyota, Liberty Mutual, JPMorgan Chase, Fannie Mae, FedEx Office, and others.

Past & Present: *Plano* is being published in 2023, as the city celebrates its sesquicentennial anniversary. Many of today's Planoites may find it difficult to envision what Plano looked like in 1873, the year the city was incorporated.

If you gaze at the gleaming high-rise towers of Legacy West, it is not easy to imagine a time when cattle and horses roamed that same land. If you work at the Plano campus of an international corporation, it's hard to comprehend that Plano's main business was once agriculture, or that the city was known as "the Mule Capital of the World." If you are waiting impatiently in traffic along Preston Road, it is difficult to picture a time when that road was the unpaved Shawnee Trail, plied by pioneers in horse-drawn wagons.

With Past & Present: *Plano*, the authors wish to help fill that gap. We hope readers will enjoy this book as a way of better understanding and appreciating present-day Plano—by picturing the Plano of the past.

# CHAPTER 1

# TRANSPORTATION

## *MULES, TRAINS, AND AUTOMOBILES*

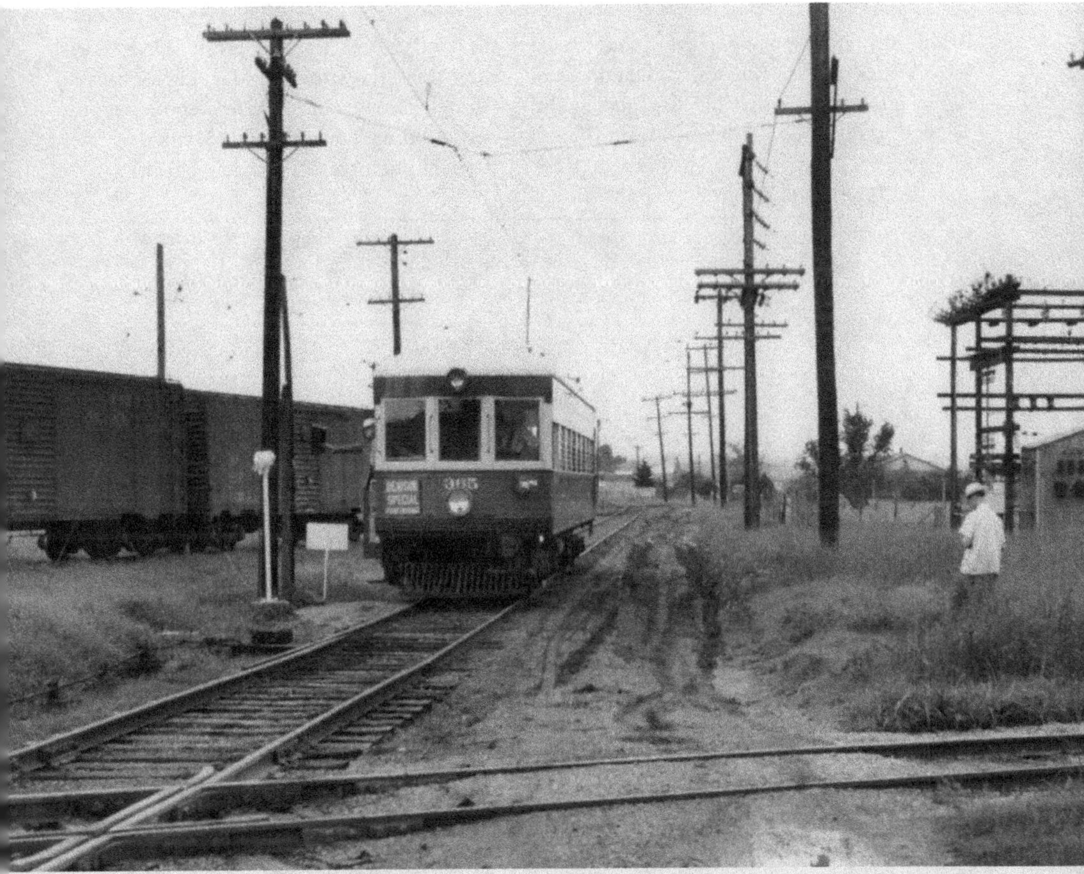

Transportation has always been destiny for Plano. The railway's arrival in 1872 transformed a pioneer outpost into a commercial center for cotton. When automobiles became widely available after World War II, Plano was again transformed into a suburb. Pictured in 1948 is the Cotton Belt and Interurban Railway crossing. (Courtesy of the Johnnie J. Myers Transportation Research Center.)

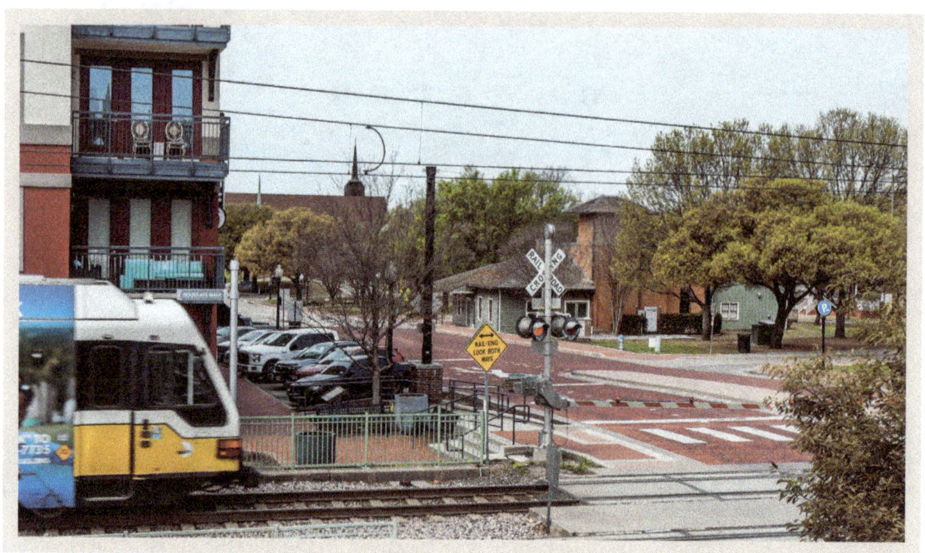

Below is a c. 1908 view of Mechanic Street (now 15th Street) looking west. The railcars in the foreground were part of the Houston and Texas Central (H&TC) Railroad; on the left is the First Christian Church, built in 1899, and the Interurban Railway station. Today, the Dallas Area Rapid Transit (DART) rail runs along the same corridor. First Christian Church remains at the same spot, but in a new building, now partially obscured by trees. (Present photograph by Jason Fehrm.)

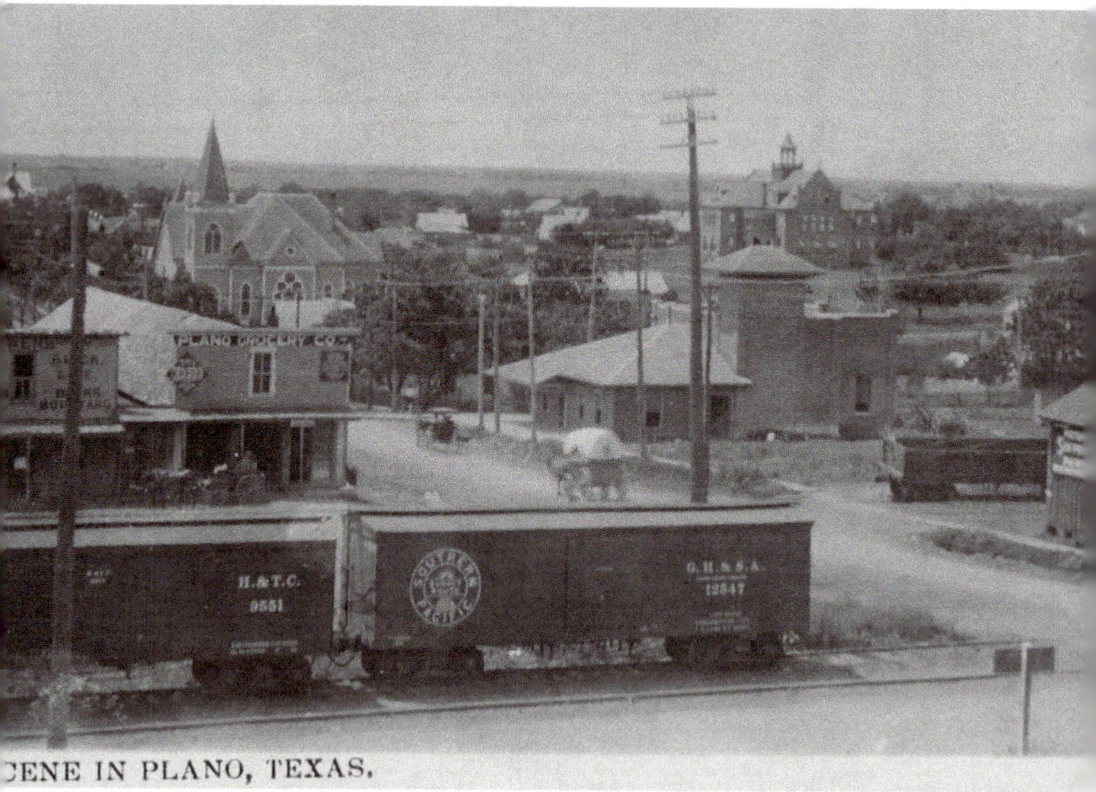

CENE IN PLANO, TEXAS.

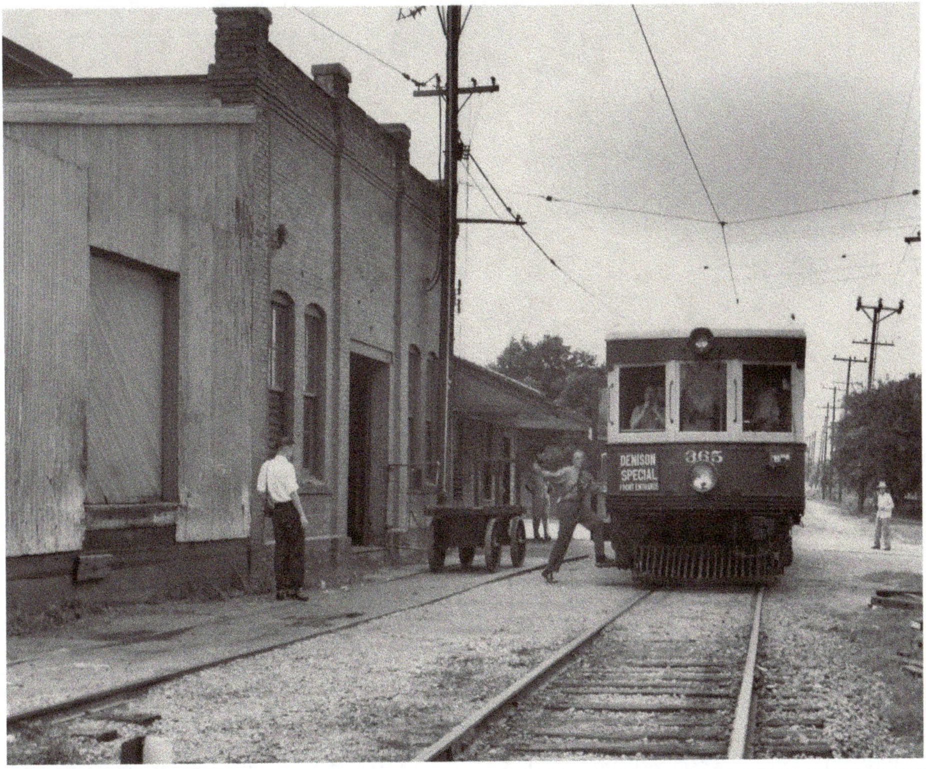

With postwar prosperity, growing availability of automobiles made the railway less viable. Pictured is a northbound Car 365 stopped at the Plano Station in 1948, the year the Interurban Railway ceased passenger operations. (Freight service continued briefly after that.) Today, a restored Car 360 sits outside the Interurban Railway Museum and is open to visitors. (Past, courtesy of the Krambles-Peterson Archives.)

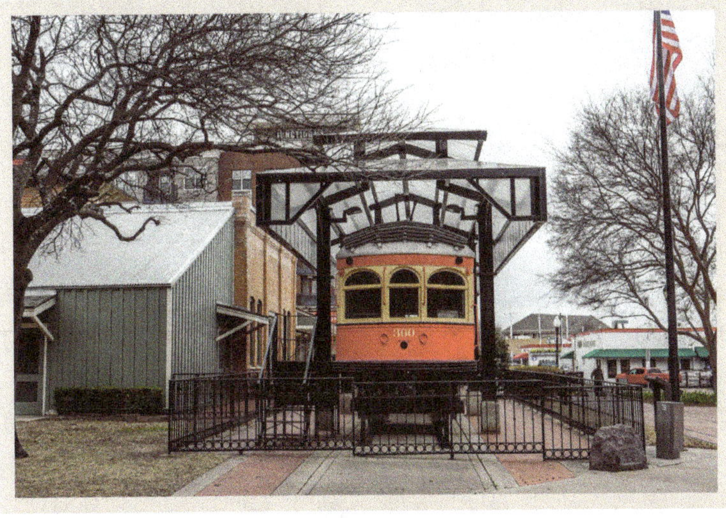

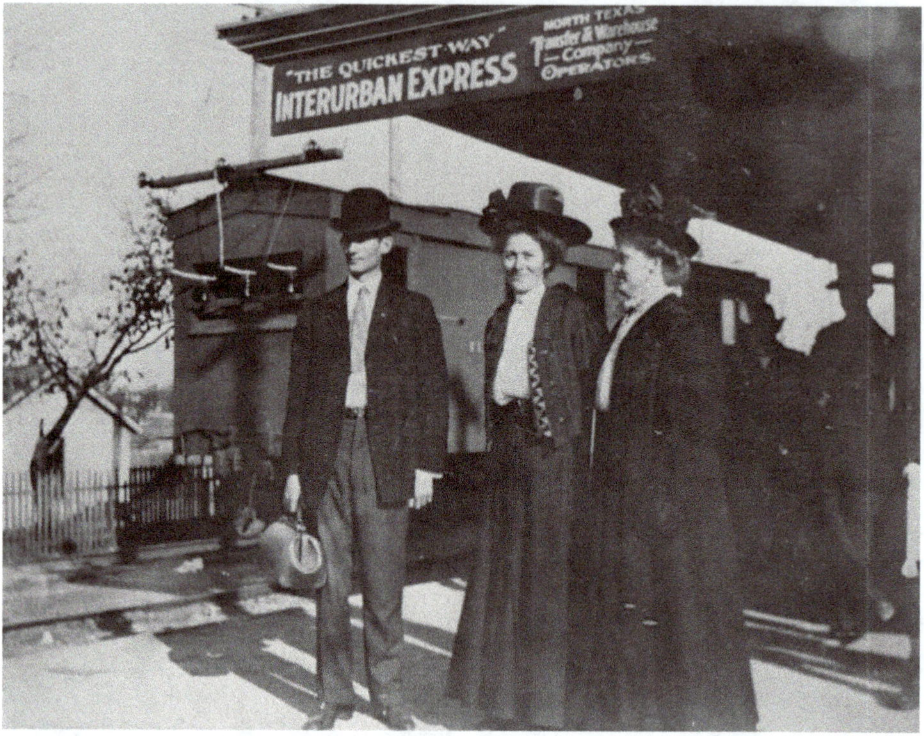

In 1908, Effie Huguley (center), her beau, C.C. Allen, and Huguley's chaperone await a Texas Traction car into Dallas at the Interurban station in downtown Plano. This vintage photograph inspired the giant painted mural now at the 15th Street DART station. Pictured in 2023, from left to right, are city manager Mark Israelson, deputy mayor pro tem Maria Tu (the first Asian American elected to Plano City Council), and Mayor John Muns.

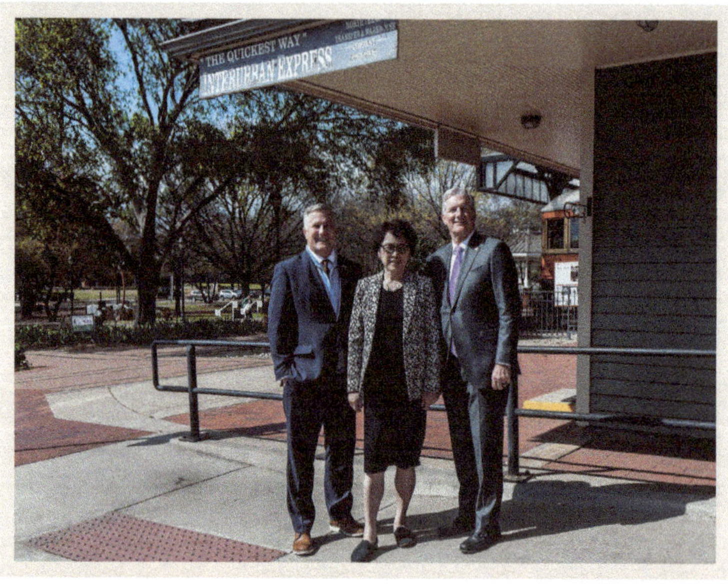

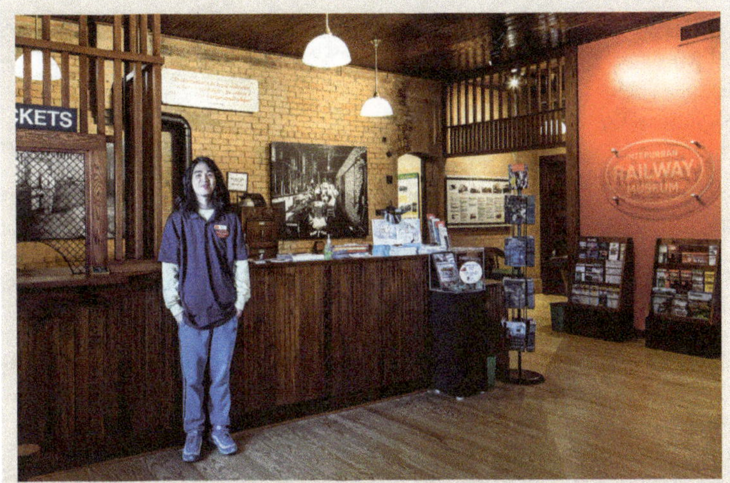


Below, this c. 1933 photograph of Dick Sheridan, station master and ticket master of the Plano Texas Electric Railway Station, was taken by his proud parents. A sign in the background says, "Do Not Spit Use Spittoon."

In 2023, intern Zhihang Zhang greets the many visitors and schoolchildren who visit the former depot, now the Interurban Railway Museum. (Past, courtesy of the Johnnie J. Myers Transportation Research Center.)

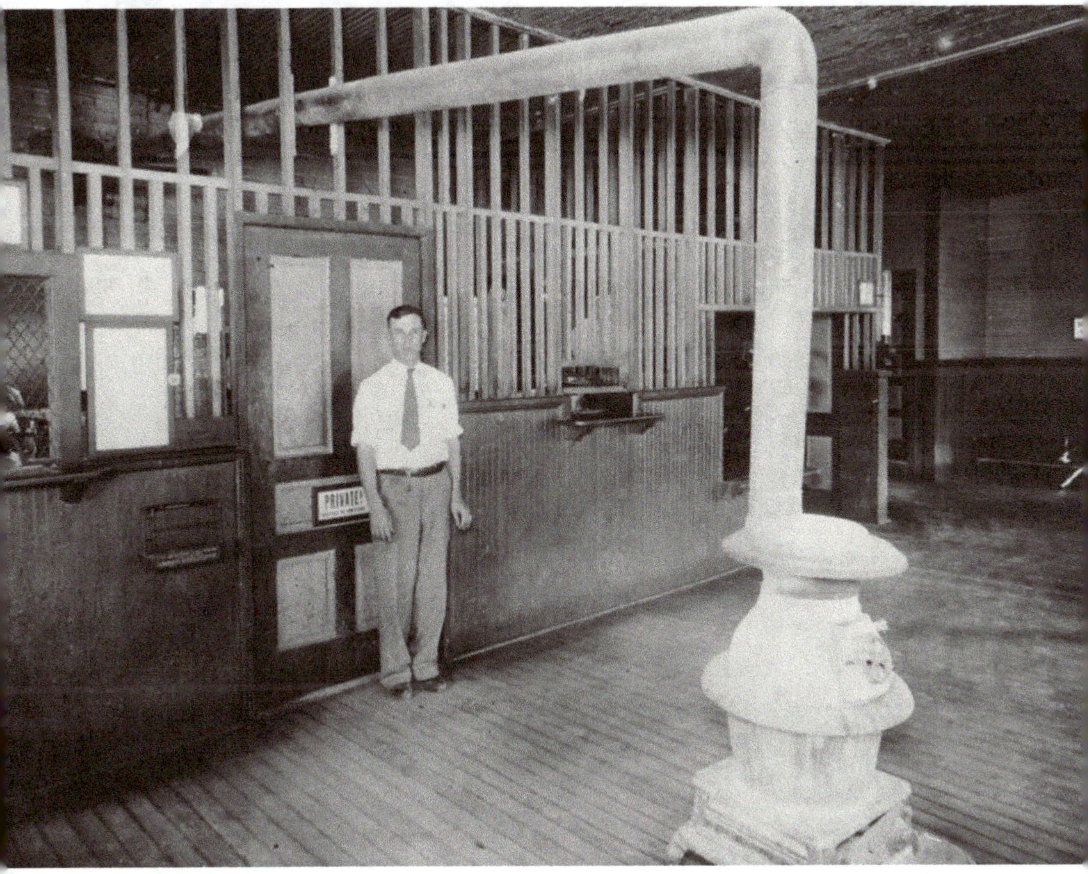

Members of the Central Electric Rail Fans Association came from as far as Massachusetts for a last ride on the Texas Electric Railway just before it ceased passenger operations in 1948. The Interurban Railway had offered service since 1908 from Denison to Dallas, Dallas to Waco, or Dallas to Corsicana. In 2023, Interurban Railway Museum staffers Terry Fleming (left) and Mike Roberts pose in the lobby area. (Past, courtesy of the Johnnie J. Myers Transportation Research Center.)

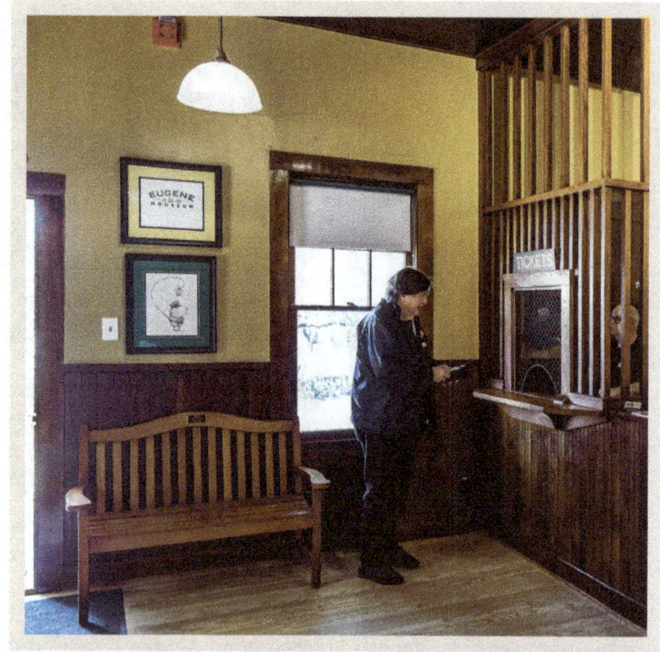

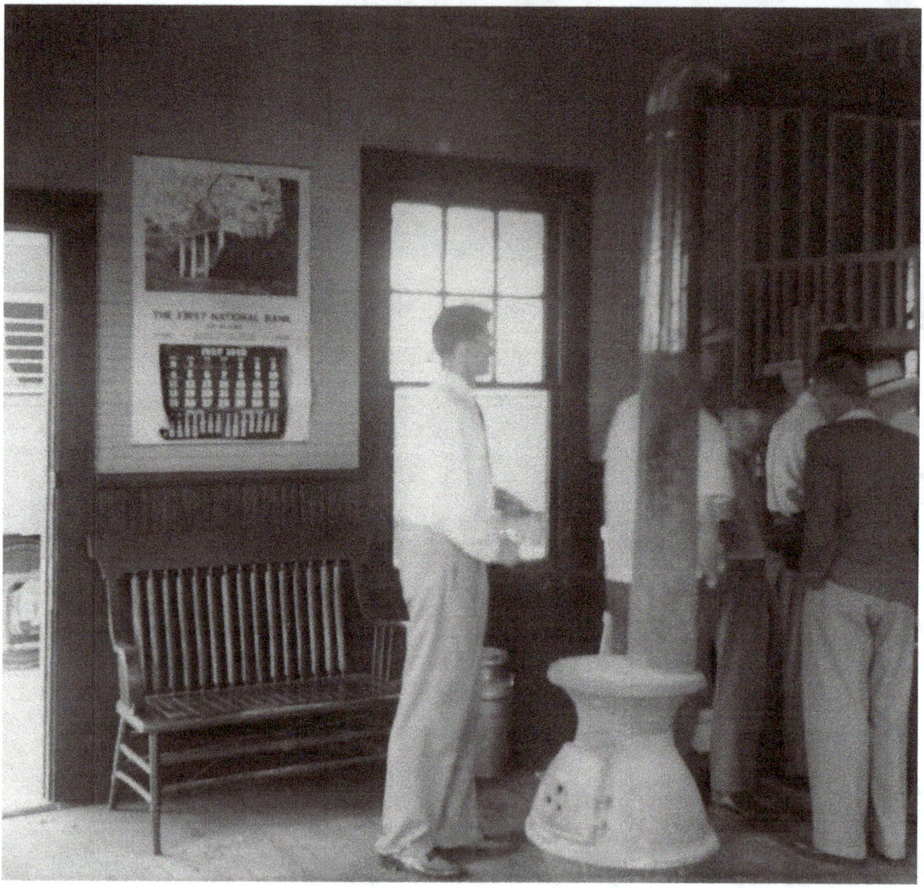

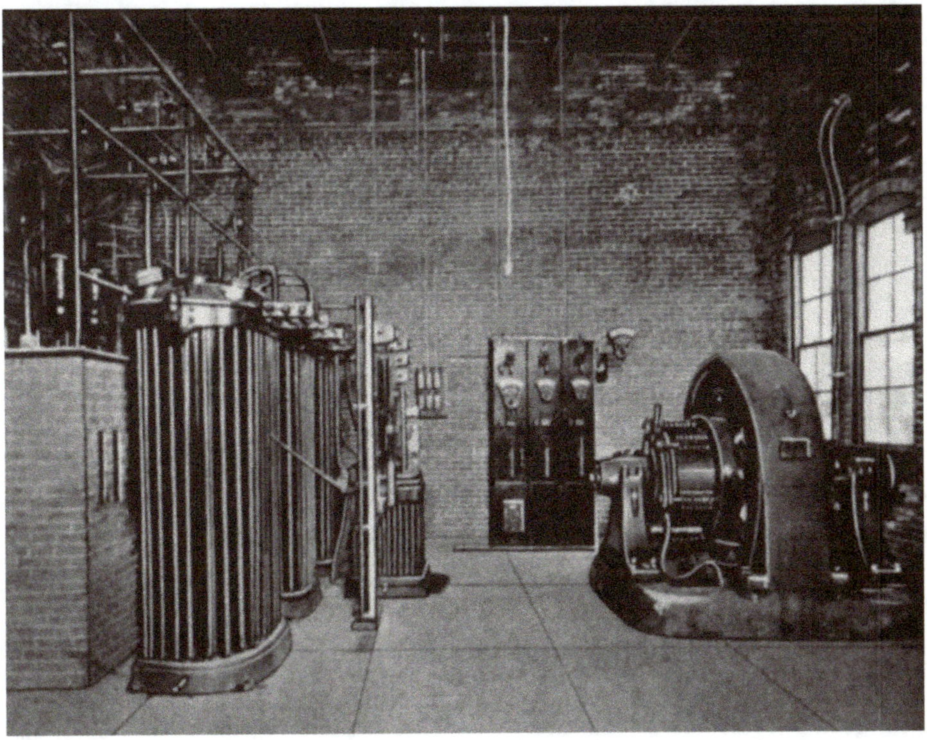

Pictured in 1907 is the interior of the Plano substation, built by Fred A. Jones Company. The new substation and depot opened in June 1908. Passengers would don their Sunday best when taking a trip on the Interurban. A one-way ticket from Plano to Dallas cost 30¢. Today, the substation is part of the display area of the Interurban Railway Museum. (Past, courtesy of Bryan Lean, North Texas History Center.)

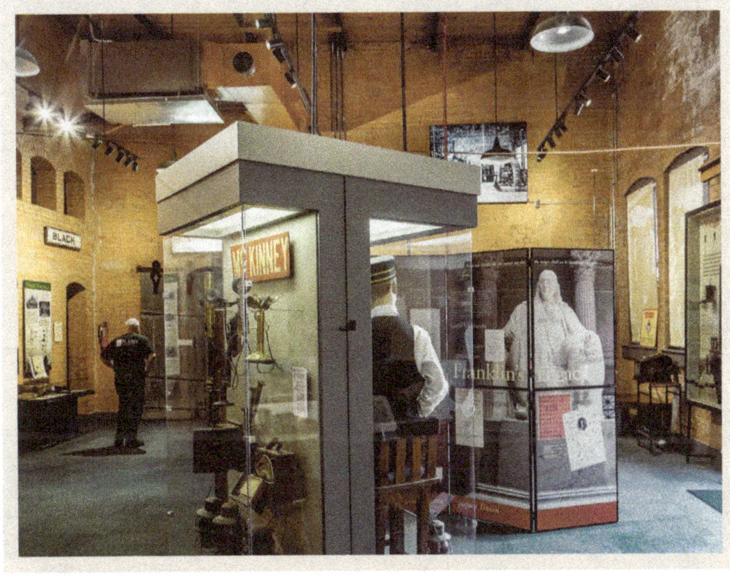

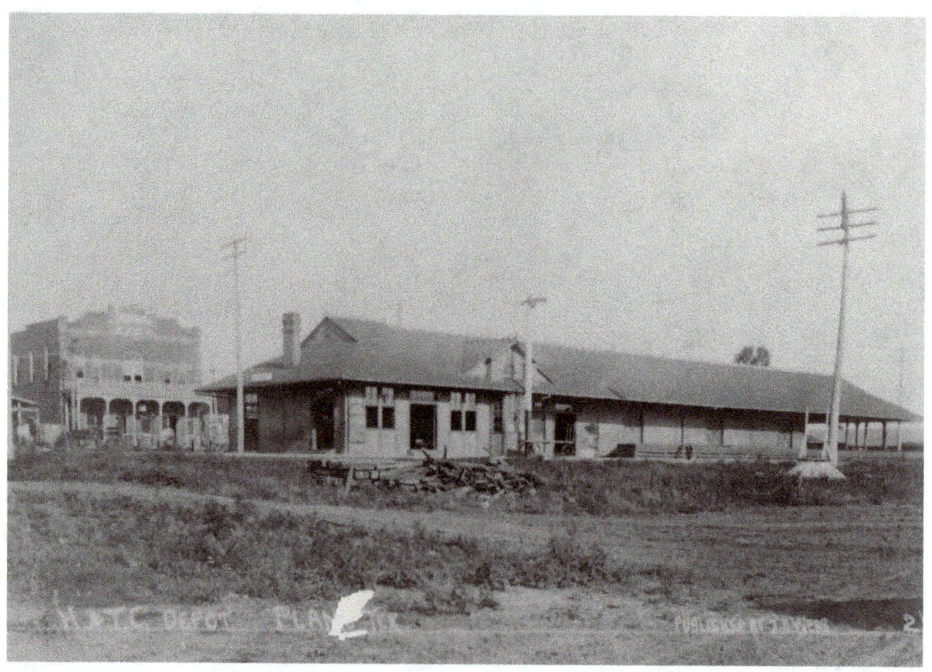

The arrival of the Houston and Texas Central Railroad in 1872 changed the community of Plano forever. Pictured is the railroad's depot in the foreground; the Moore House Hotel (left) provided lodging for travelers passing through by train. The Masonic Lodge acquired and renovated the Moore House in 1925. The lodge is still active at that same location today at 1414 J Avenue. Today, the DART rail travels along the same path as the H&TC.

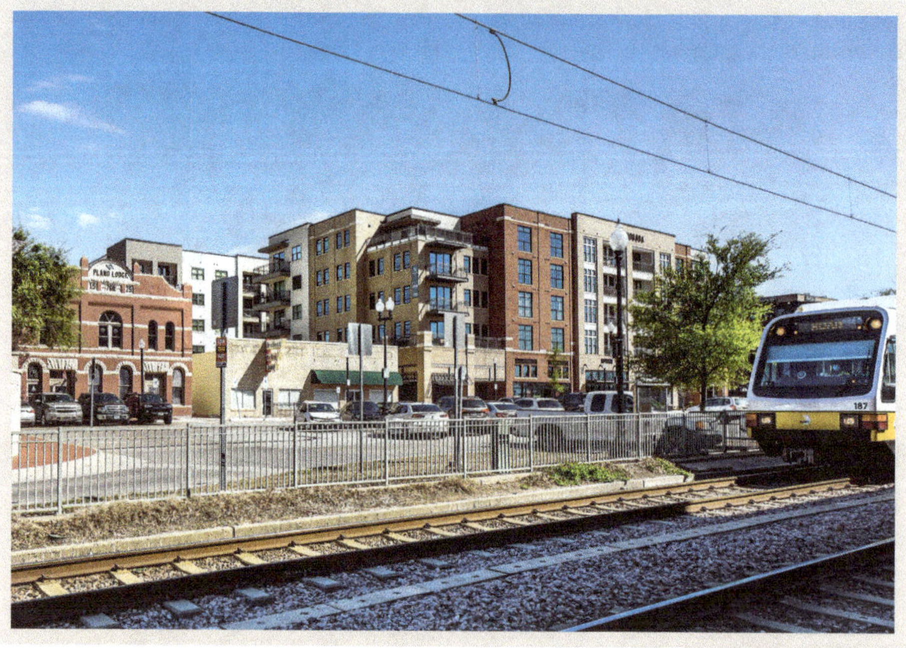

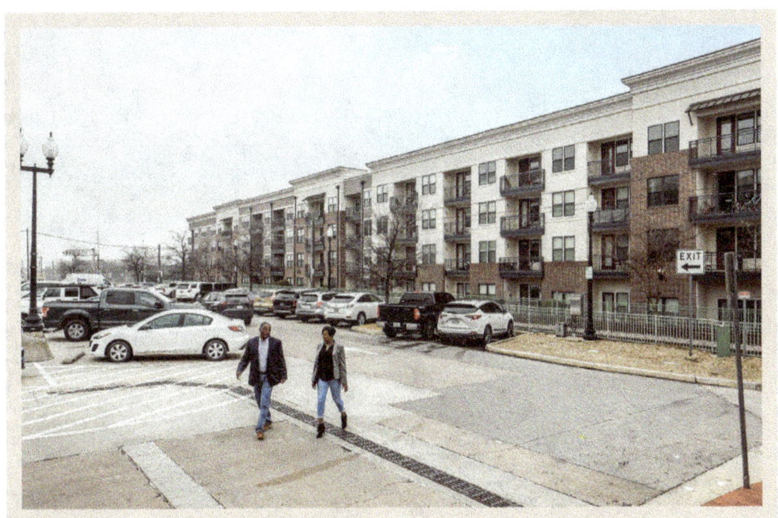


Just a year after the arrival of the H&TC Railroad, the city of Plano was incorporated and platted in a traditional grid pattern oriented to the tracks. The vintage photograph shows the building that originally served as the H&TC depot, later converted to Plano Implement Company. Today, Junction 15 apartments occupy the area. Pictured are Shun and James Thomas, grandson of James Lawrence Thomas (1890–1968), a prominent Plano citizen, humanitarian, and namesake of Thomas Elementary.

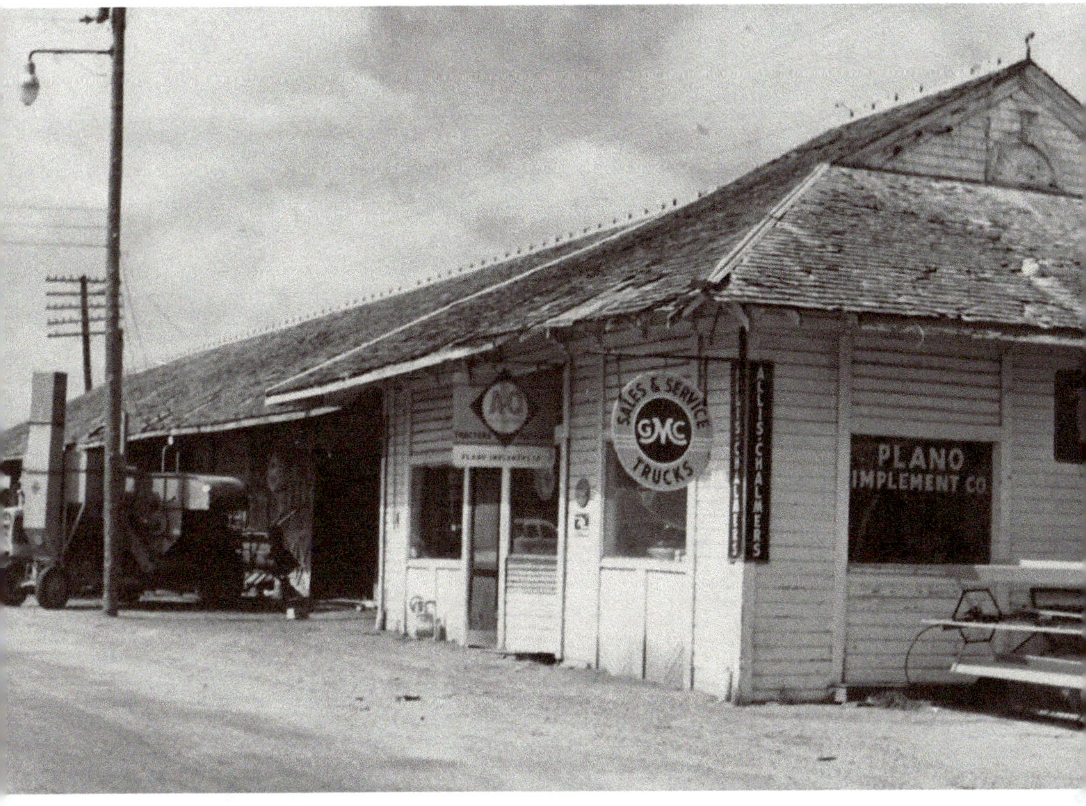

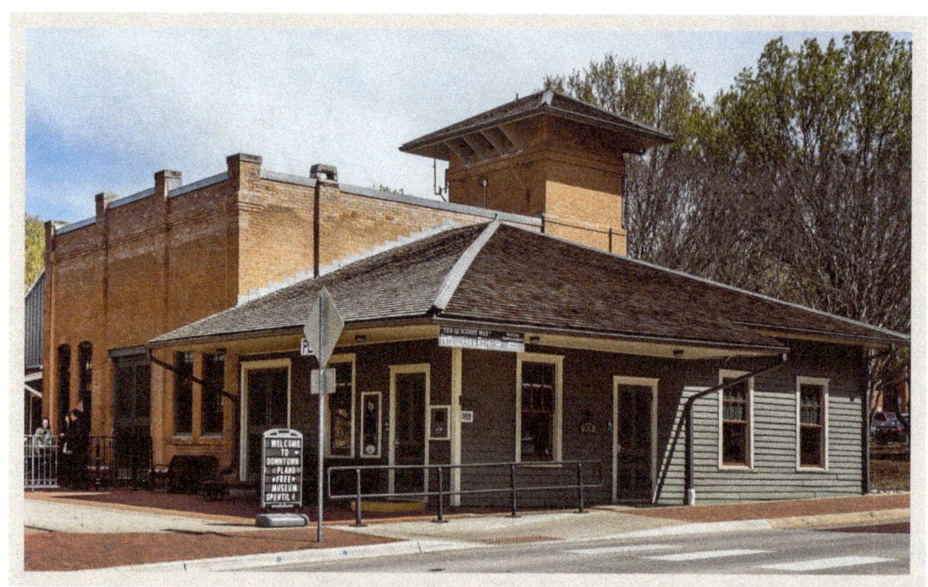


After the Interurban Railway ceased passenger operations in 1948, the Plano station was closed. For the next 40 years or so, the building was occupied by multiple businesses, including a lawn mower repair shop. (Past, courtesy of the Johnnie J. Myers Transportation Research Center.

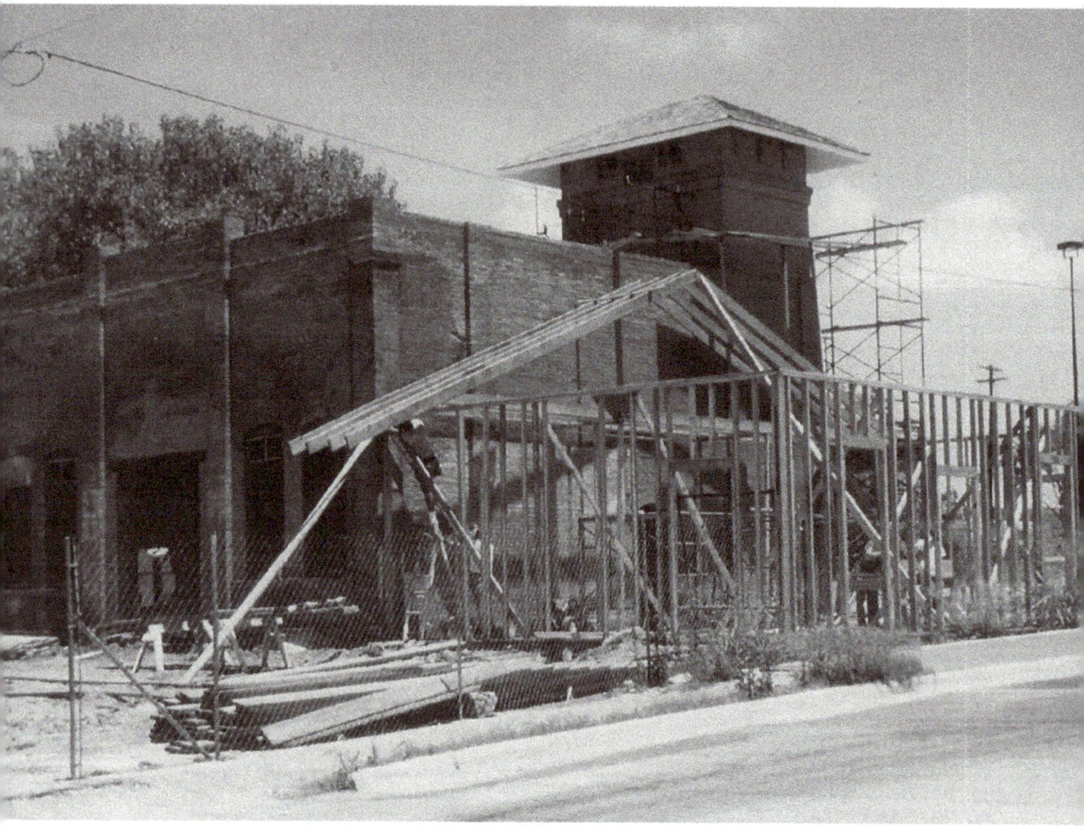

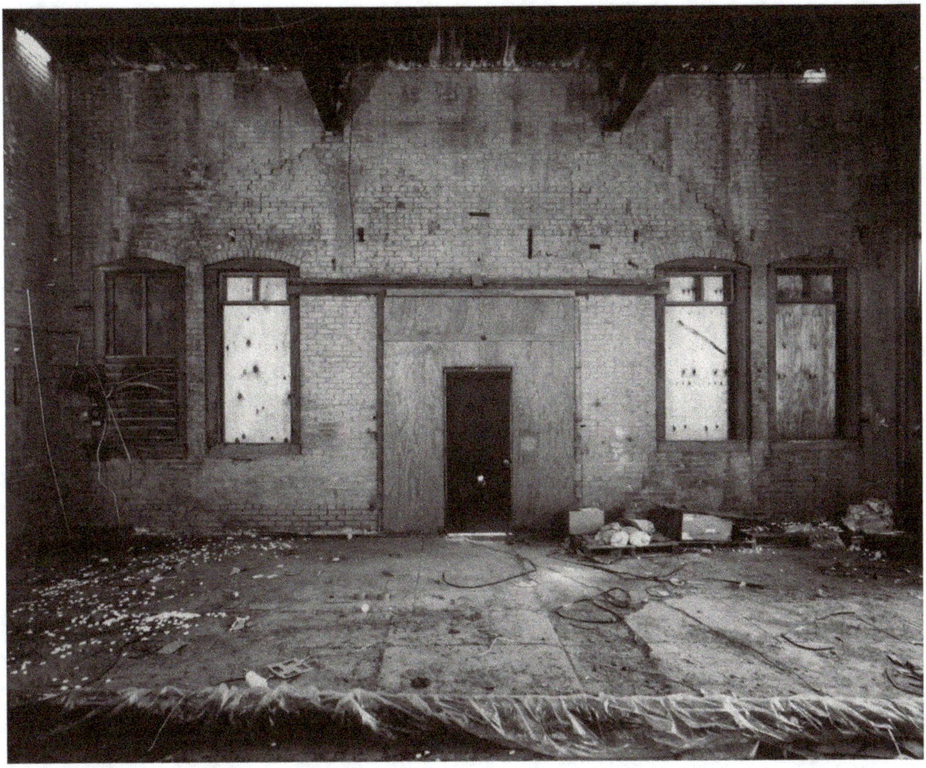

In 1983, renovation of the former Interurban Railway Plano station began. The city of Plano purchased the building and developed it into the Interurban Railway Museum, located next to the DART rail station and Haggard Park in downtown Plano. (Past, courtesy of Johnnie J. Myers Transportation Research Center.)

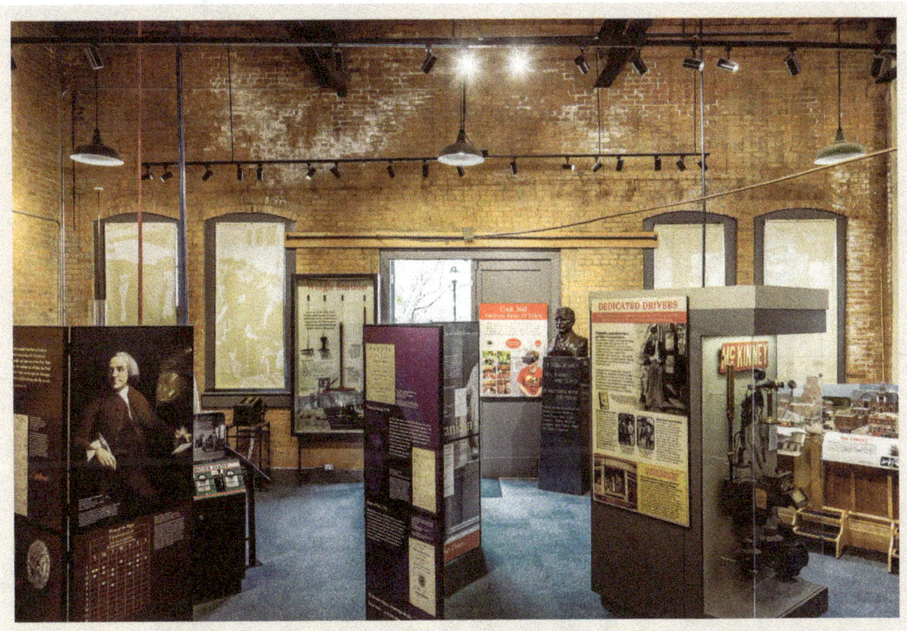

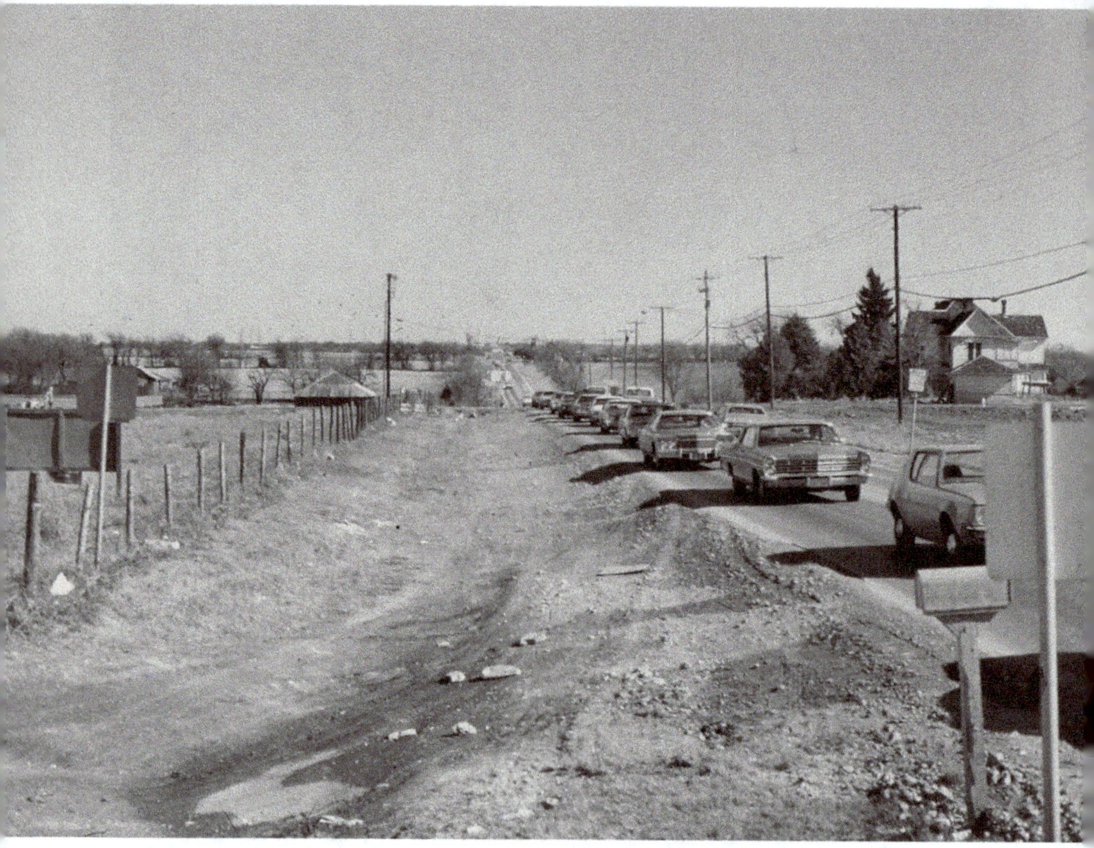

The Farrell-Wilson House (upper right) was surrounded by farmland in the 1970s. Roads were congested even before the city's population boom. Ammie Wilson (1880–1972) occupied the house until her death, bringing fame to Plano with her prizewinning Hampshire sheep. Today, the house is part of the Heritage Farmstead Museum at 1900 West 15th Street. The area is fully developed, with strip shopping centers, retail businesses, and homes filling the former farmland. (Past, courtesy Plano Parks & Recreation Department.)

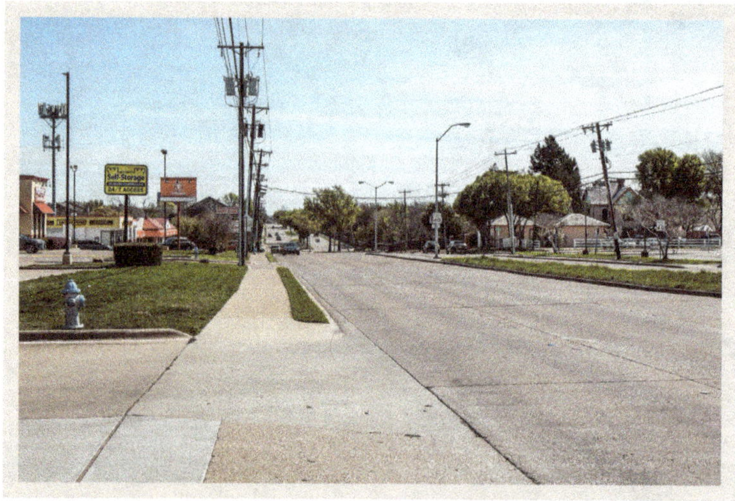

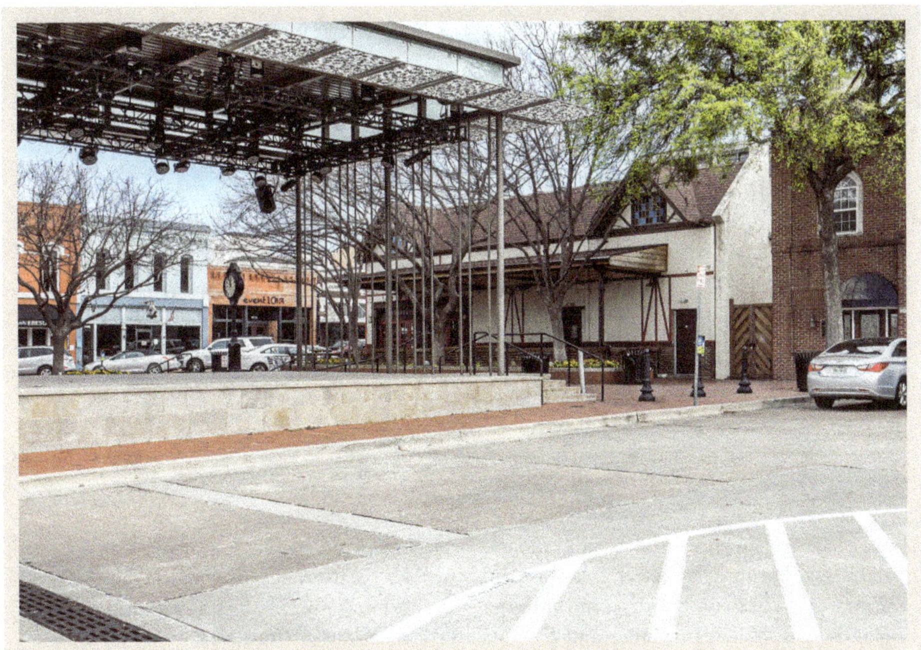

Plano resident James Gilbreath snapped this photograph of his cousin's customized Pontiac Trans Am in 1977 and then had the film developed at Harrington Pharmacy (center). Today, McCall Plaza occupies much of the parking lot. The plaza was dedicated in 1986 as part of the Texas Sesquicentennial and overhauled, with the addition of a stage, in 2016. The karate studio is now office space, and The Fillmore Pub is in the former pharmacy location. (Past, courtesy of James Gilbreath.)

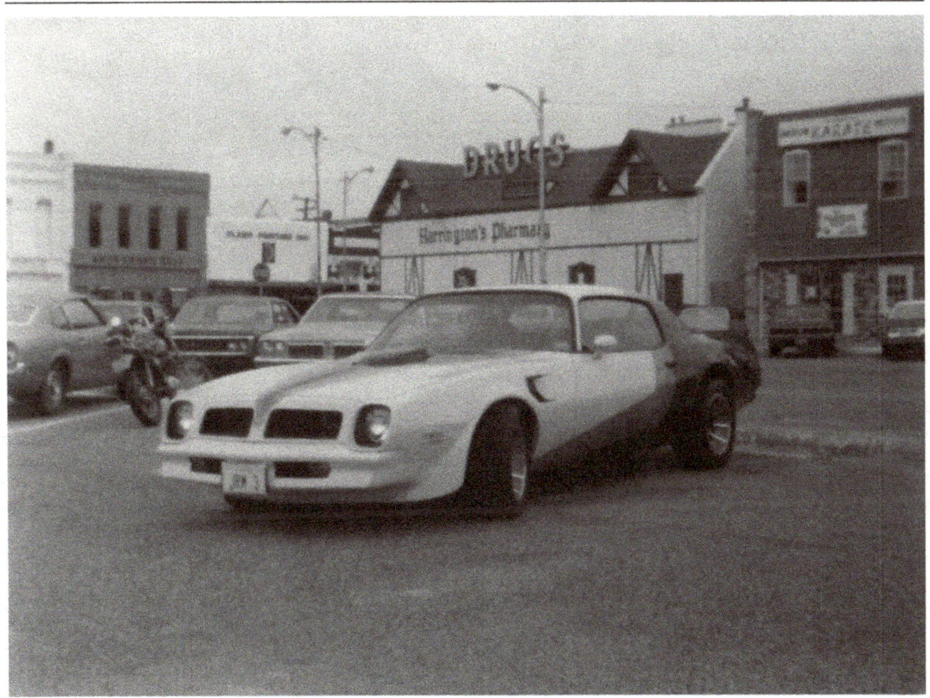

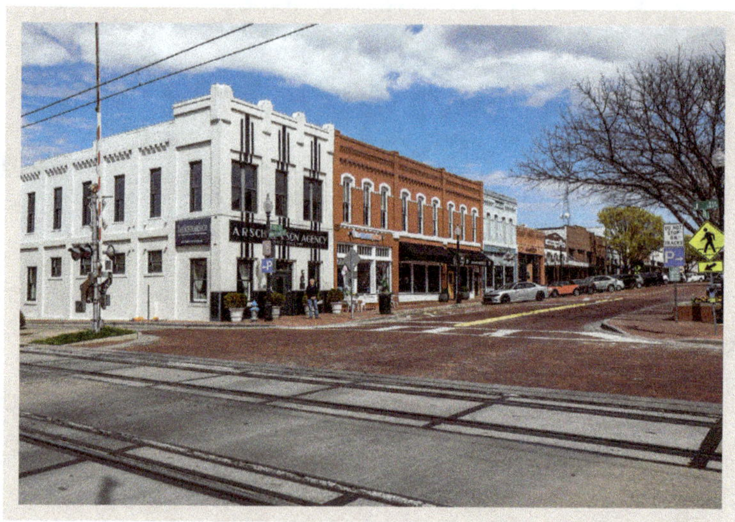

After fire destroyed most of downtown Plano in 1895, the Plano National Bank was still standing and soon rebuilt. Today, the building is home to A.R. Schell Insurance and remains at the corner of 15th Street and the DART rail. Pictured in front is owner Jamie Schell, whose great-grandfather Fred Schimelpfenig arrived in Plano in 1878 and served as Plano's mayor from 1901 to 1908.

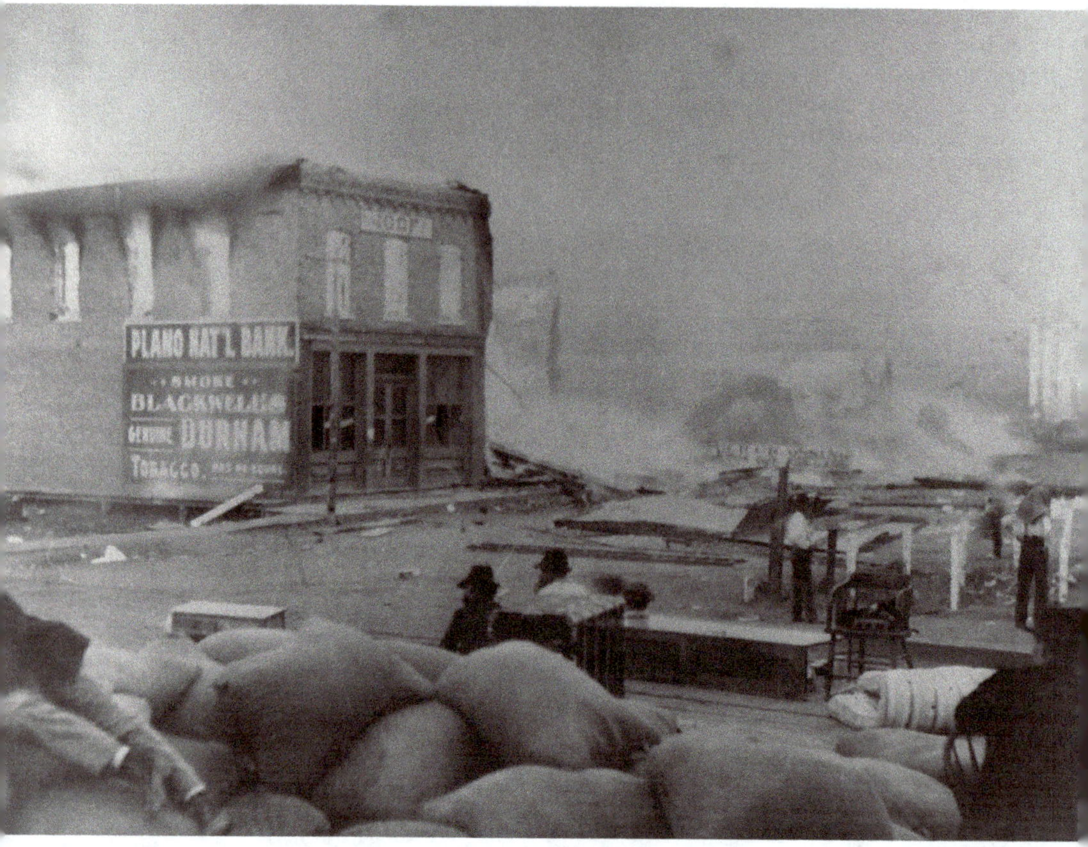

# CHAPTER 2

# DOWNTOWN

## *STORES, SHOPS, COTTON, AND CATTLE*

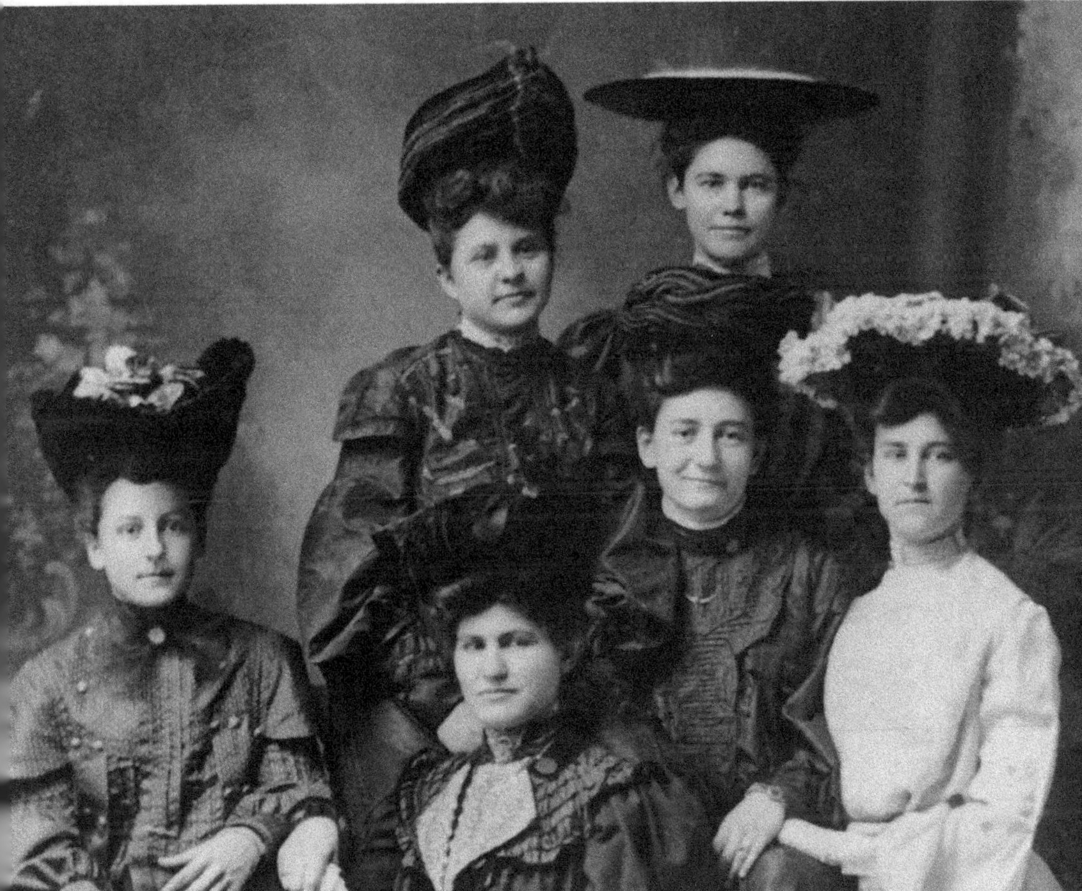

Going downtown once meant dressing up in one's finest. This February 1904 photograph shows a group of Plano ladies on their way to Clara Schimelpfenig's party. Pictured from left to right are Bessie Shepard Shelton, Bess Tamer Gray, Mamie Fortner Johnston, Anna Hood Chaddick, Maude Goode Shepard, and Gutha Mathews Hood.

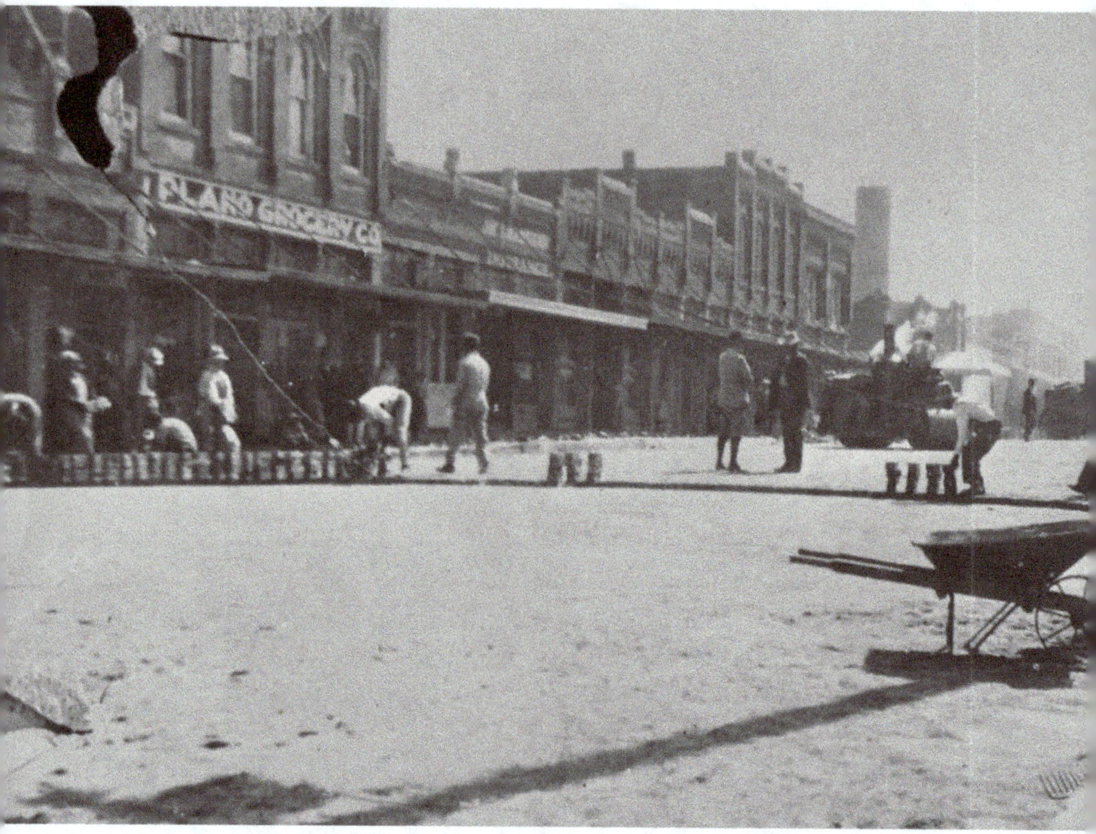

Workers repair Mechanic Street in downtown Plano. Before paving, engine oil was sprayed on dirt roads to contain the dust. By 1925, Mechanic Street—now 15th Street—was paved. Paving the streets was a major step forward in establishing Plano's modern infrastructure. Downtown streets were especially essential for transporting goods to the stores to sell to the citizens.

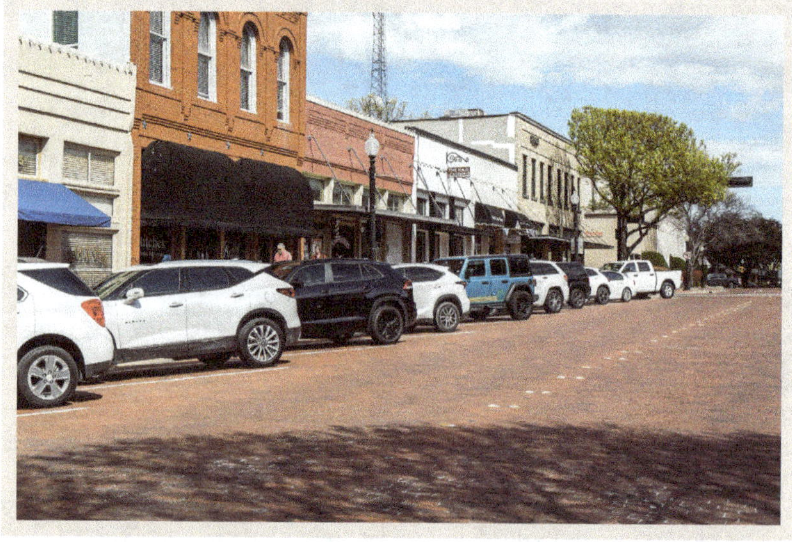

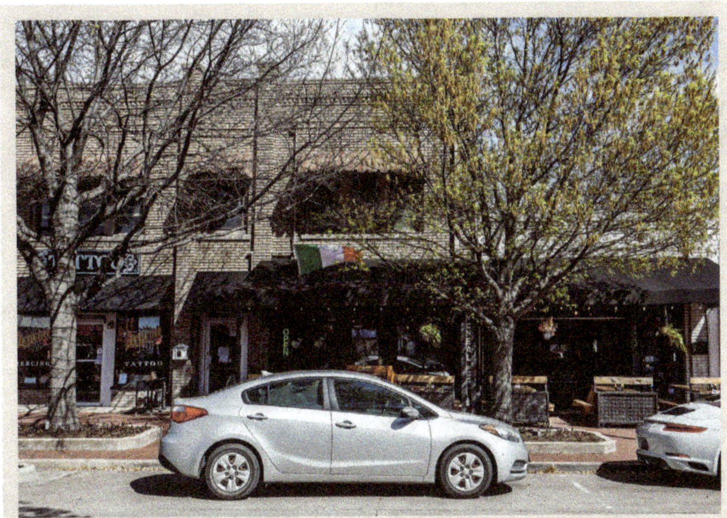

In 1958, Rite-Way Cleaners was located on the southeast corner of K Avenue and 15th Street in downtown Plano. Note the words "Rooms" in the brick—the building also offered hotel rooms. Today, Legend Tattoo & Piercing Shop and McNeal's Tavern occupy the buildings. The door in the middle is the entrance to the Las Brisas Inn, which continues to offer budget accommodations.

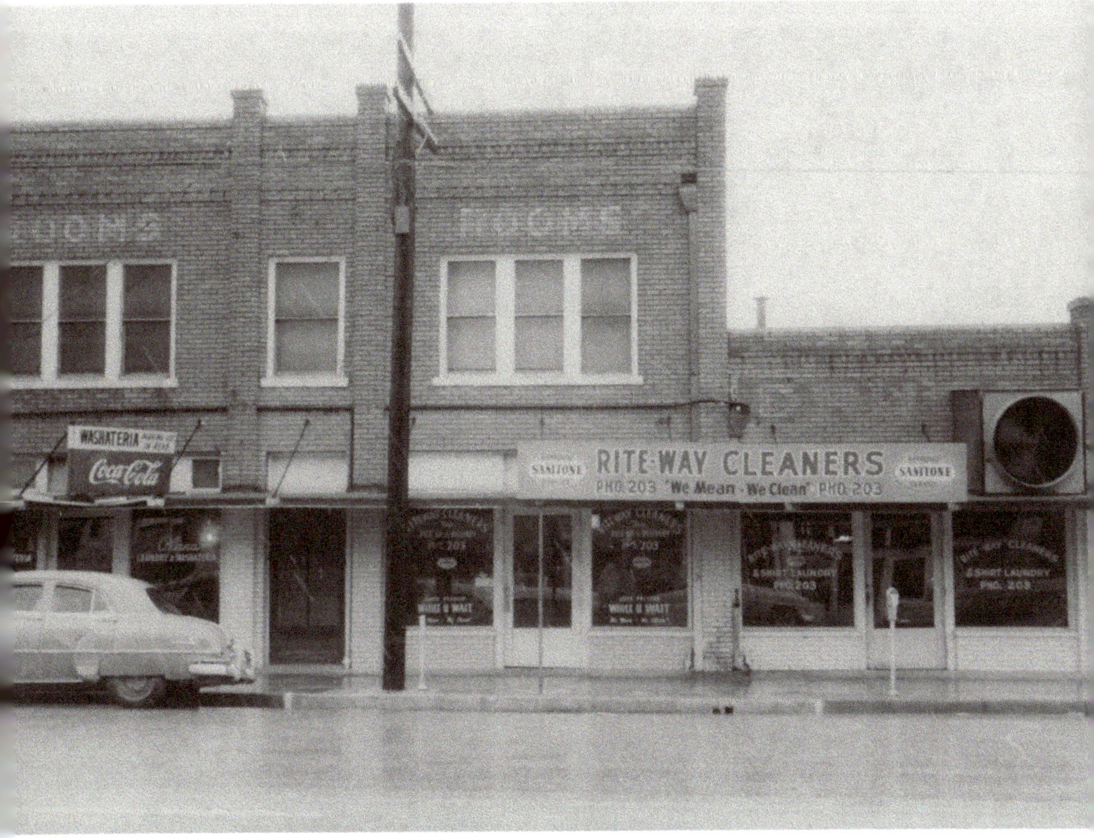

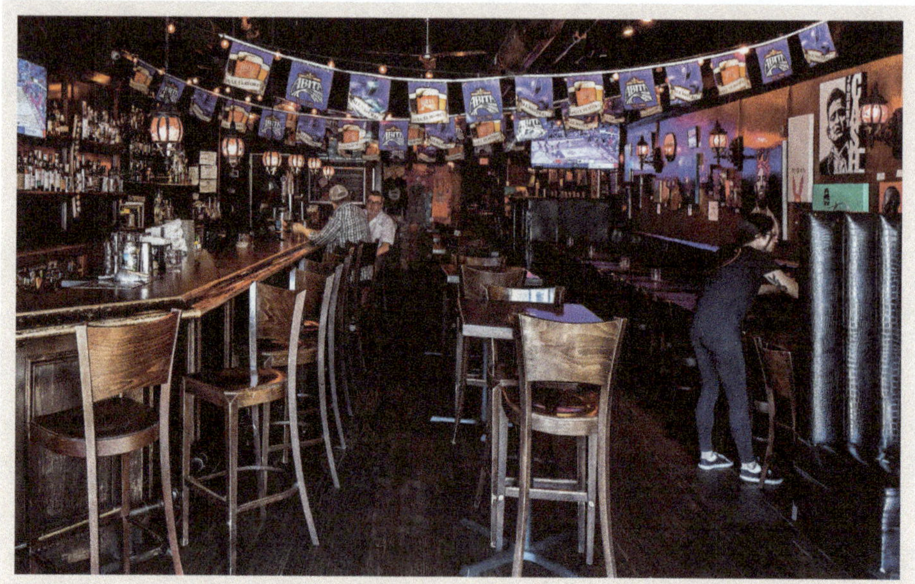

The Carpenter Pharmacy was owned by E.A. Carpenter, a graduate of the Philadelphia College of Pharmacy. In 1899, when the photograph was taken, druggists sold paints and oils, wallpaper, and many other products in addition to medications. Today, the space at 1011 East 15th Street is occupied by Vickery Park Plano, a popular bar and eatery.

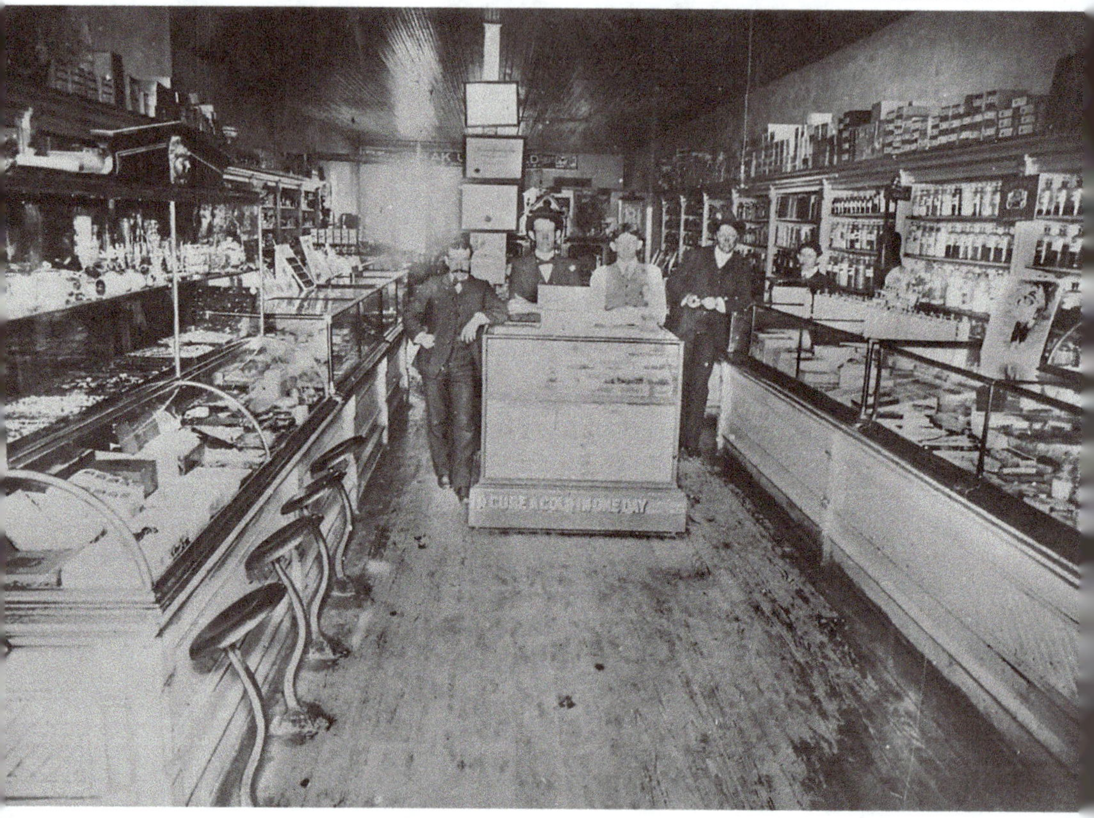

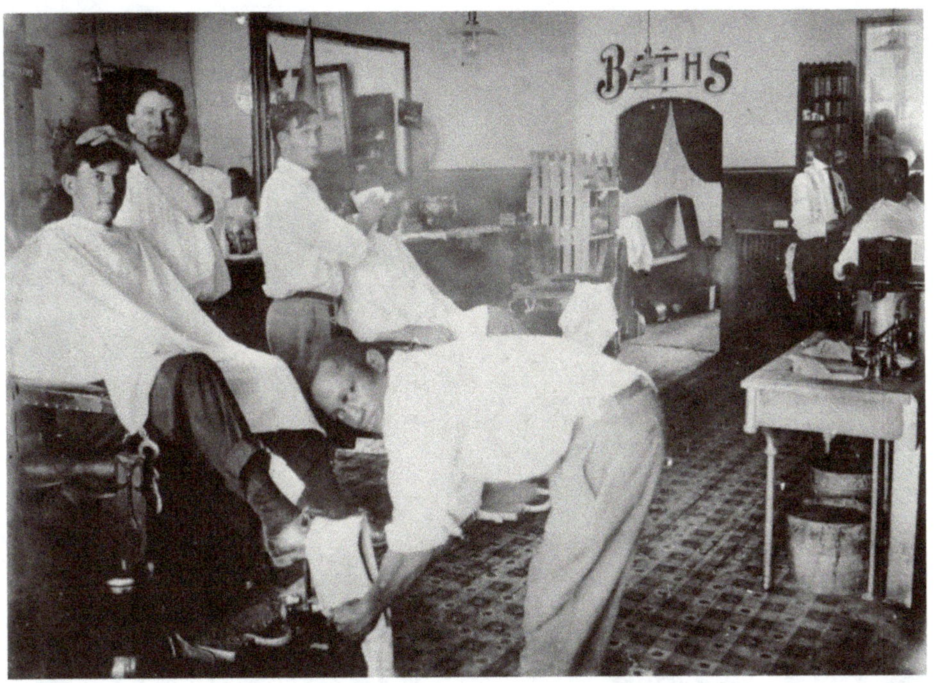


Starting in 1895 until the early 1940s, downtown Plano was buzzing with activity every second Monday of the month, dubbed "Trades Days." Families came by wagon or horseback to buy and sell livestock and farm machinery. Merritt Barber Shop was especially busy on Trades Days, as men came in for a haircut and a bath. (Notice the sign for baths in the back in the c. 1920s photograph.) Today, Lemma Coffee occupies the Merritt Building at 1023 East 15th Street.

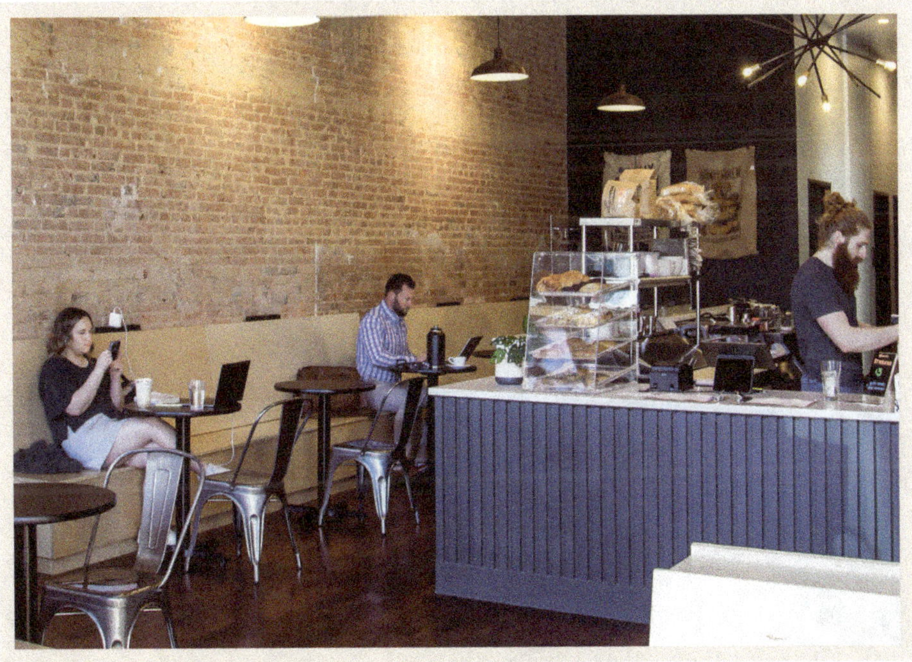

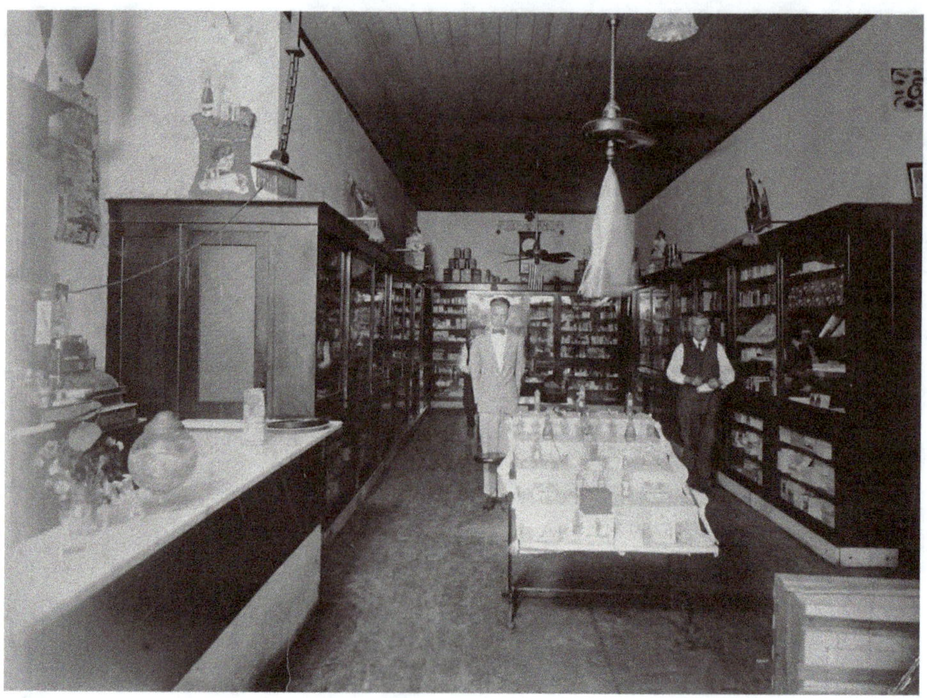

Members of the Harrington family have been active in Plano businesses since Mary Elizabeth Harrington, widow of Silas Harrington, arrived in 1881. The S.M. Harrington Drug Store, in this c. 1910 photograph, shows Robert Harrington (left) and S.M. Harrington. The Harrington family still owns commercial property in downtown Plano. Today, the space is an eatery, Better than Sex Desserts, at 1010 East 15th Street. Pictured in front are Sheila and Derrick Miller, owners of the historic building and restaurant.

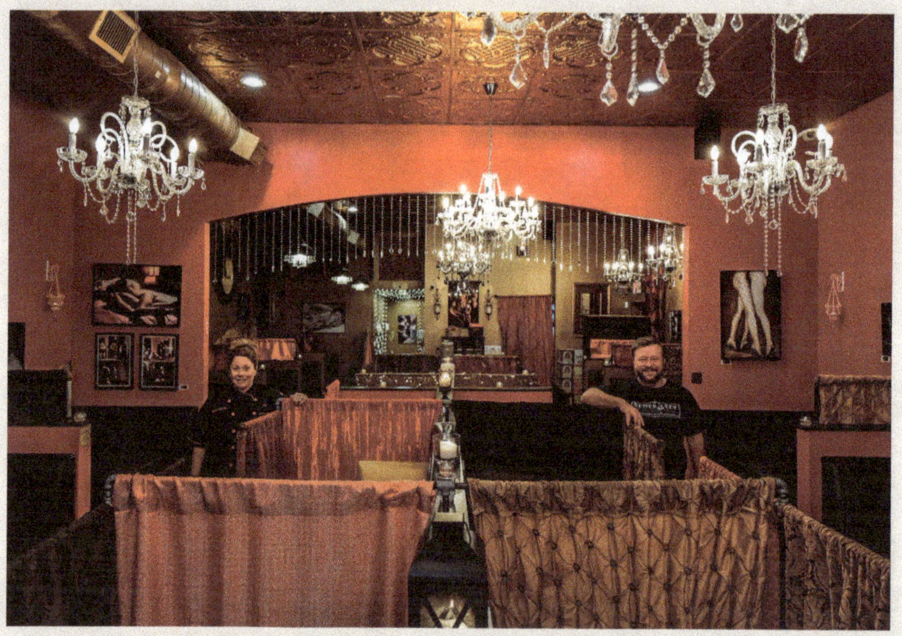

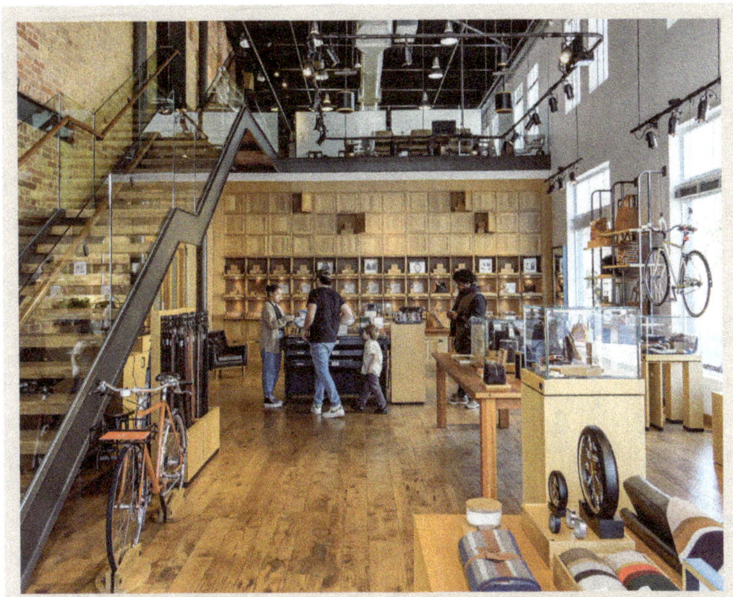

Harrington Furniture and Undertaking occupied the building at the northwest corner of 15th Street and K Avenue from 1893 until the 1980s. E.O. Harrington's name is still visible in the tile floor at the entrance. Today, Shinola occupies the building, selling fine watches, leather goods, and more.

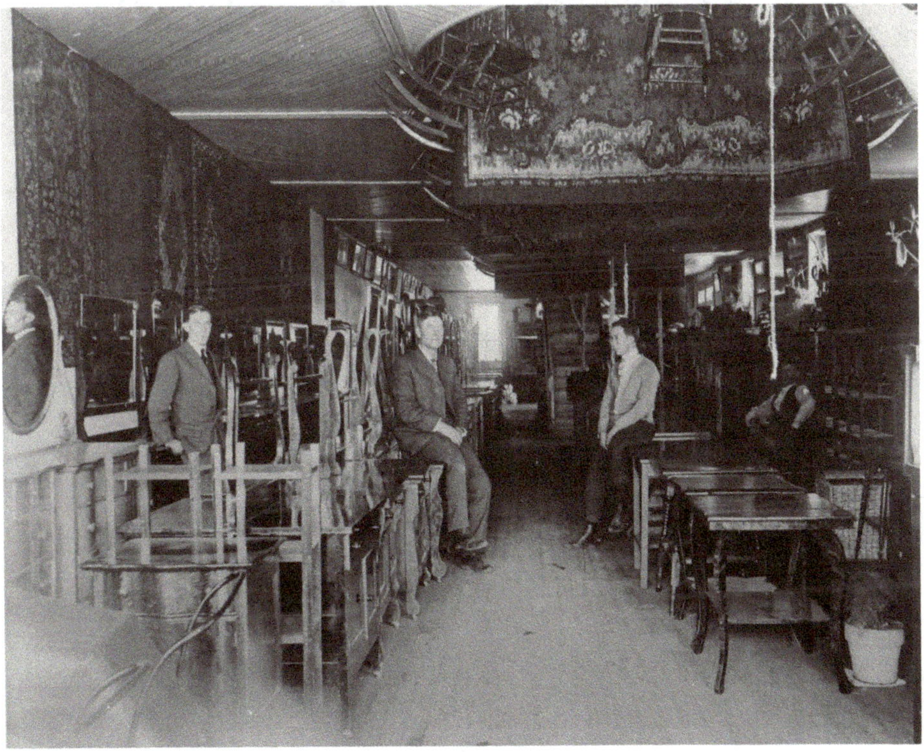

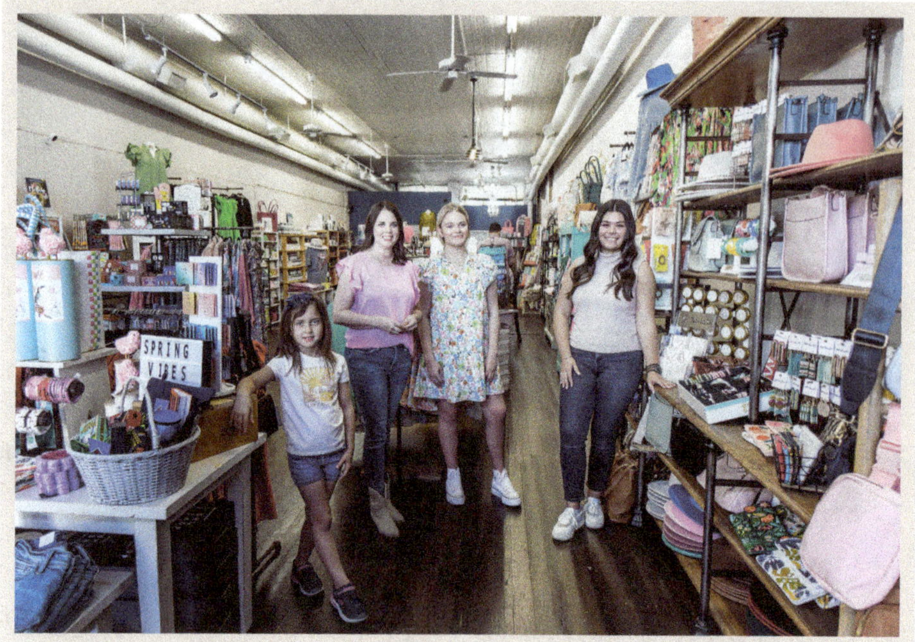


"In 1960, Moore's Variety Store on 15th Street was every child's dream—toys galore and Archie comic books, which we all collected," according to longtime resident Rick Saigling. Today, the space at 1024 East 15th Street is occupied by Lyla's Clothing, Décor & More. Pictured from left to right are Cambrie Wauters (the owner's daughter), shop owner Meagan Wauters, Lyla's employee Kennedi Grimes, and shopper Emily Hurd.

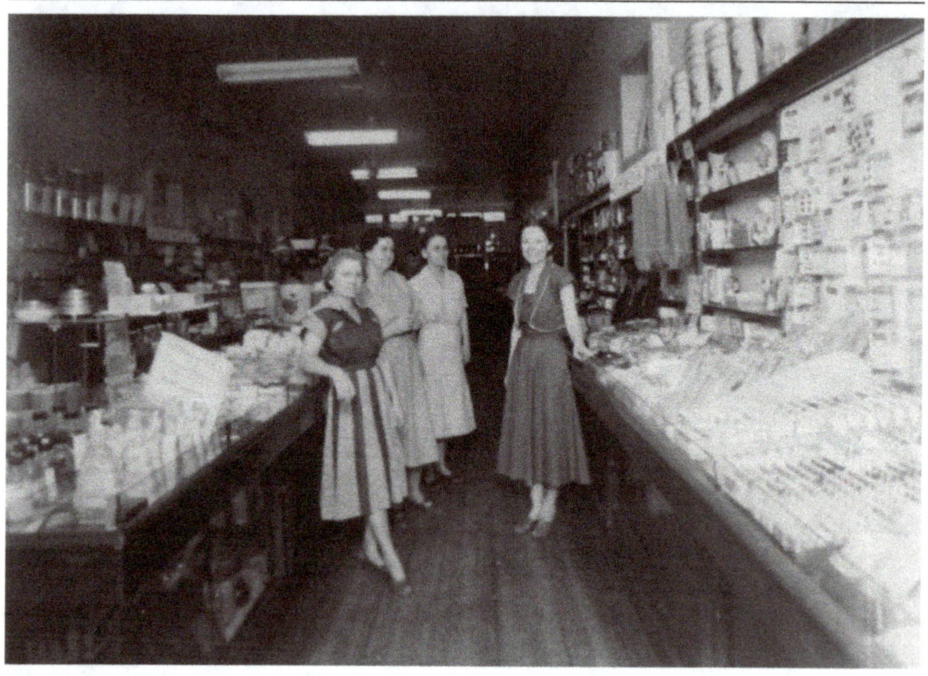

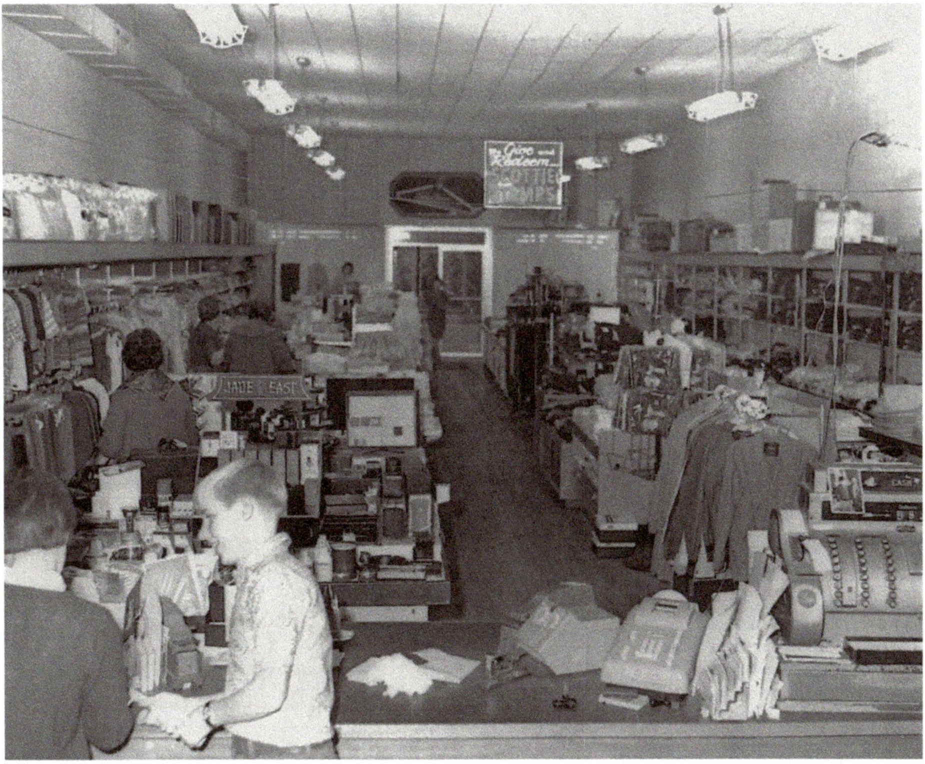

The space at 1013 East 15th Street was home to three different department stores from 1906 until the 1960s. The Mathews Store carried home goods as well as fancy hats for the young ladies, made by local milliners Nancy Mathews and her daughters, Ollie and Theo. Next, Federated Department Stores occupied the building, followed by Nathan White Department Store (pictured) in the 1960s. Today, the space is a party and meeting venue, event1013. (Present, courtesy of Ron Pierce.)

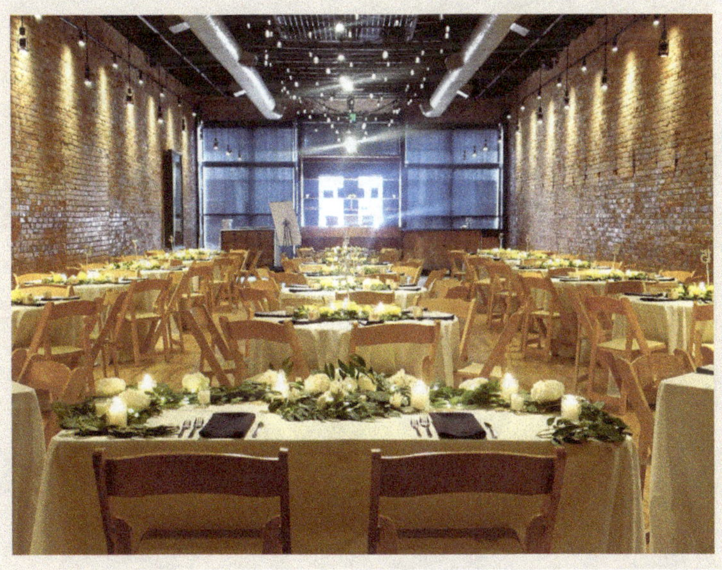

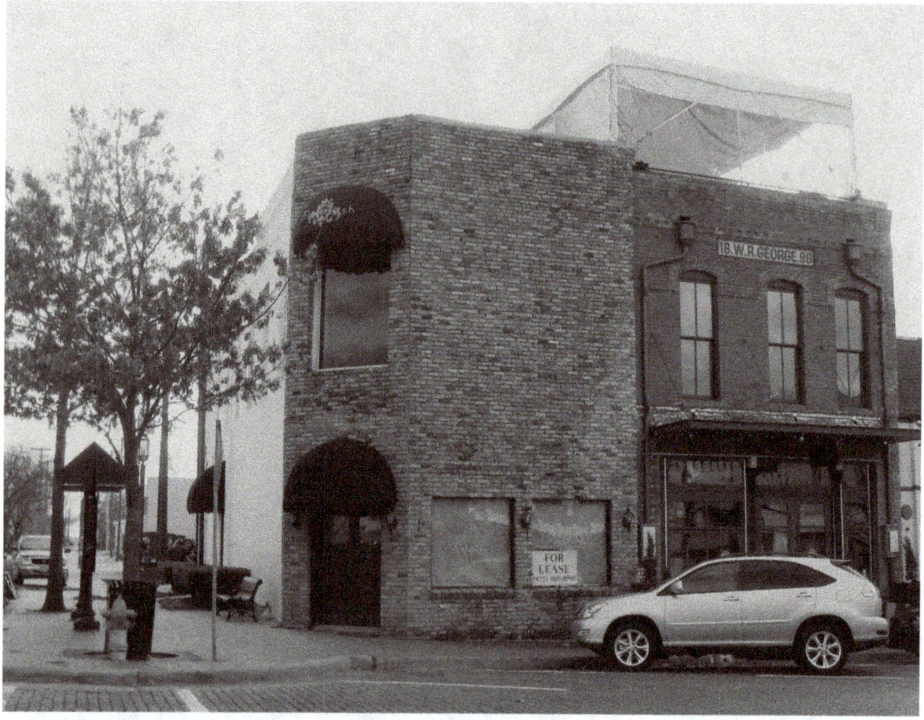

This 1896 structure was originally a wagon shop, then a salon, then Mayes Café. In the 1960s, owners added cloaking—a common practice as downtown businesses sought to lure customers away from the malls. Love Photography occupied the building in the early 2000s. Around 2010, new owners removed the old façade to uncover the original brick and Art Deco embellishments. Today, La Foofaraw occupies the space at 1008 East 15th Street. (Past, courtesy of the City of Plano.)

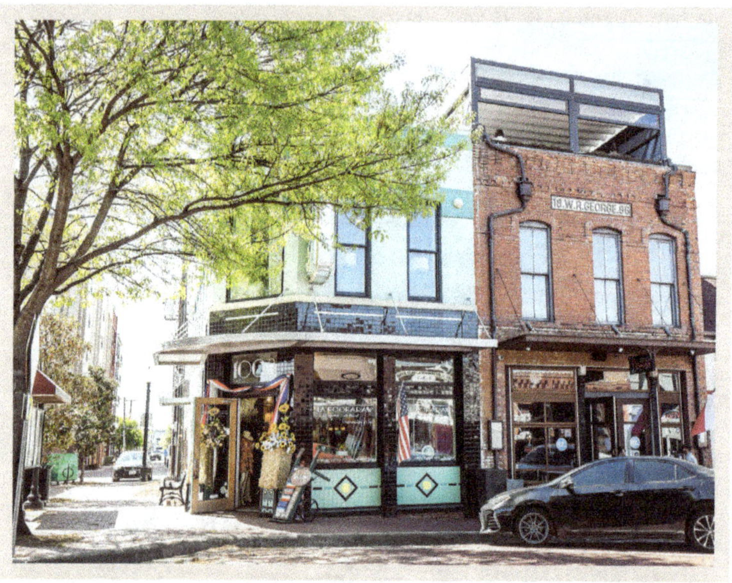

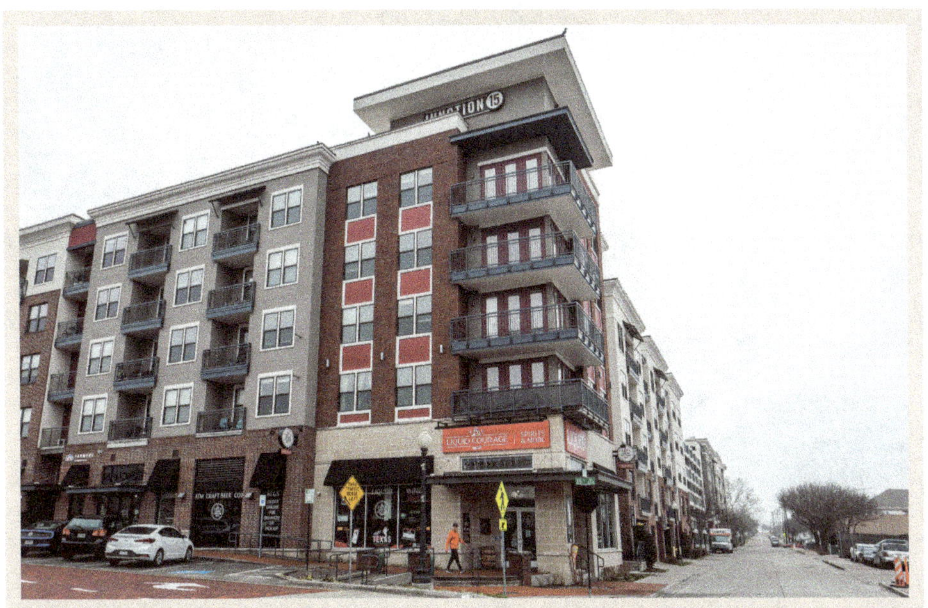


Brothers Henry B. Carlisle and J.M. Carlisle came from Tennessee in 1889 to open a grocery store in downtown Plano, which sold grain, hay, and cottonseed as well as fancy and staple groceries. Henry B. Carlisle is third from right in this 1910 photograph. The store was later named Plano Grocery Co. Hard times led to the store's closing during the Depression. Today, the Junction 15 Apartments occupy the corner of 15th Street and I Avenue, where Carlisle Grocery once stood.

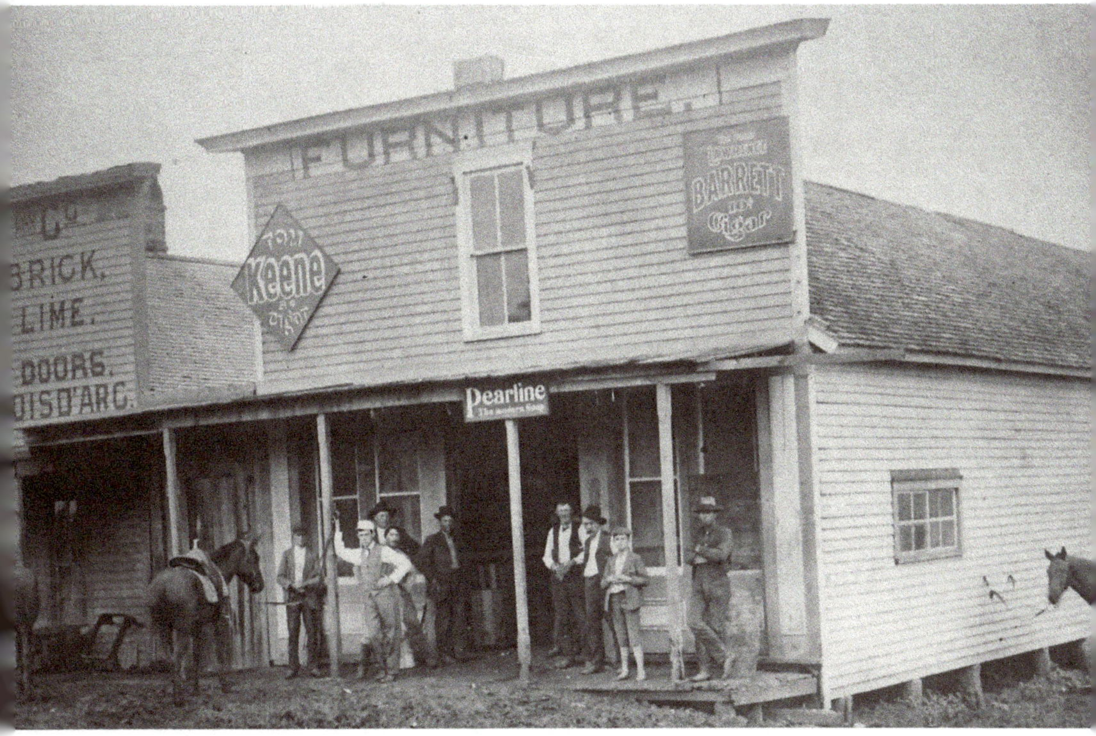

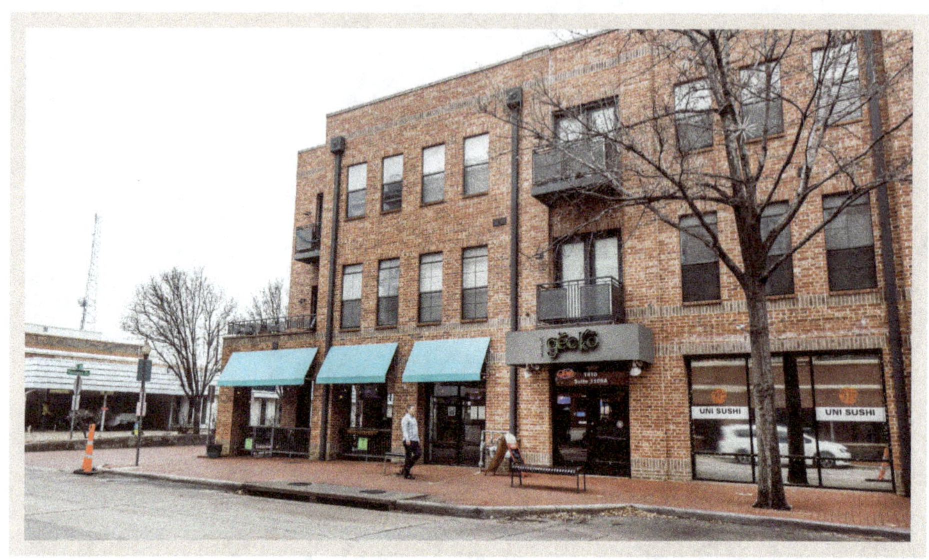


The Plano Hotel, shown around 1915, provided accommodations for travelers who arrived by way of the railways. Owned and operated by George A. Kisler and Janie Kisler, the hotel was located on the east side of K Avenue, between 14th and 15th Streets. Today, the area is occupied by Café Gecko Eastside.

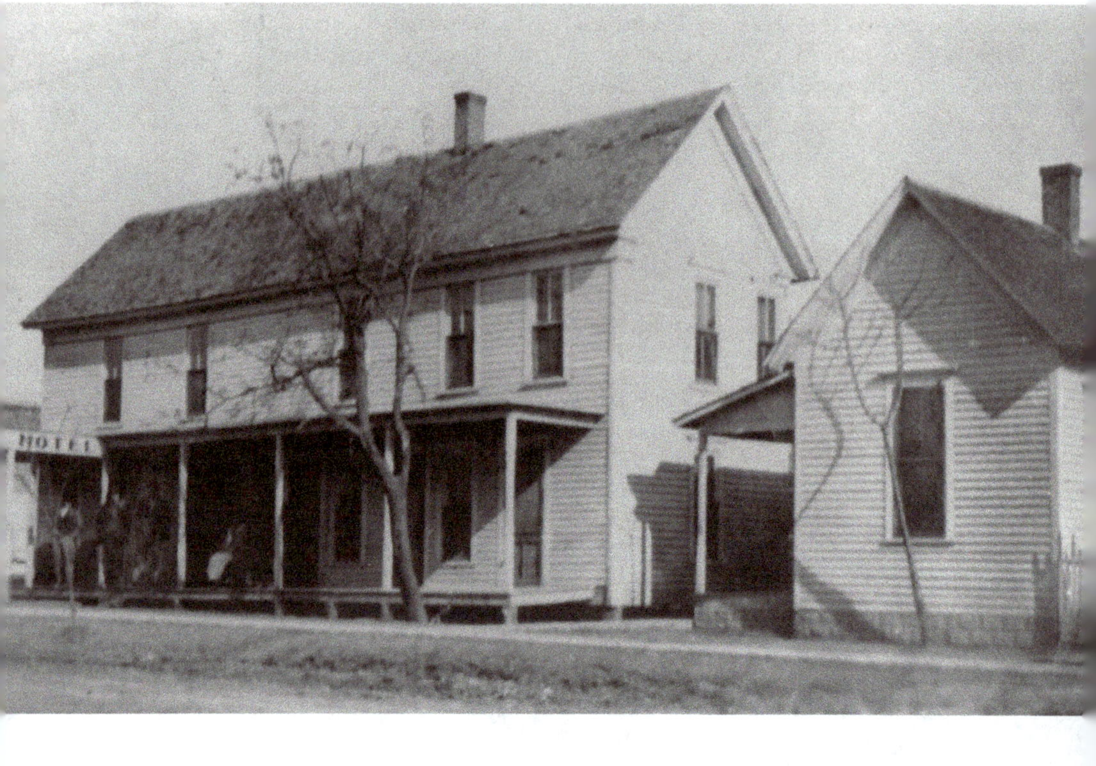

# Chapter 3

# Agriculture
## *Plano's Rural Roots*

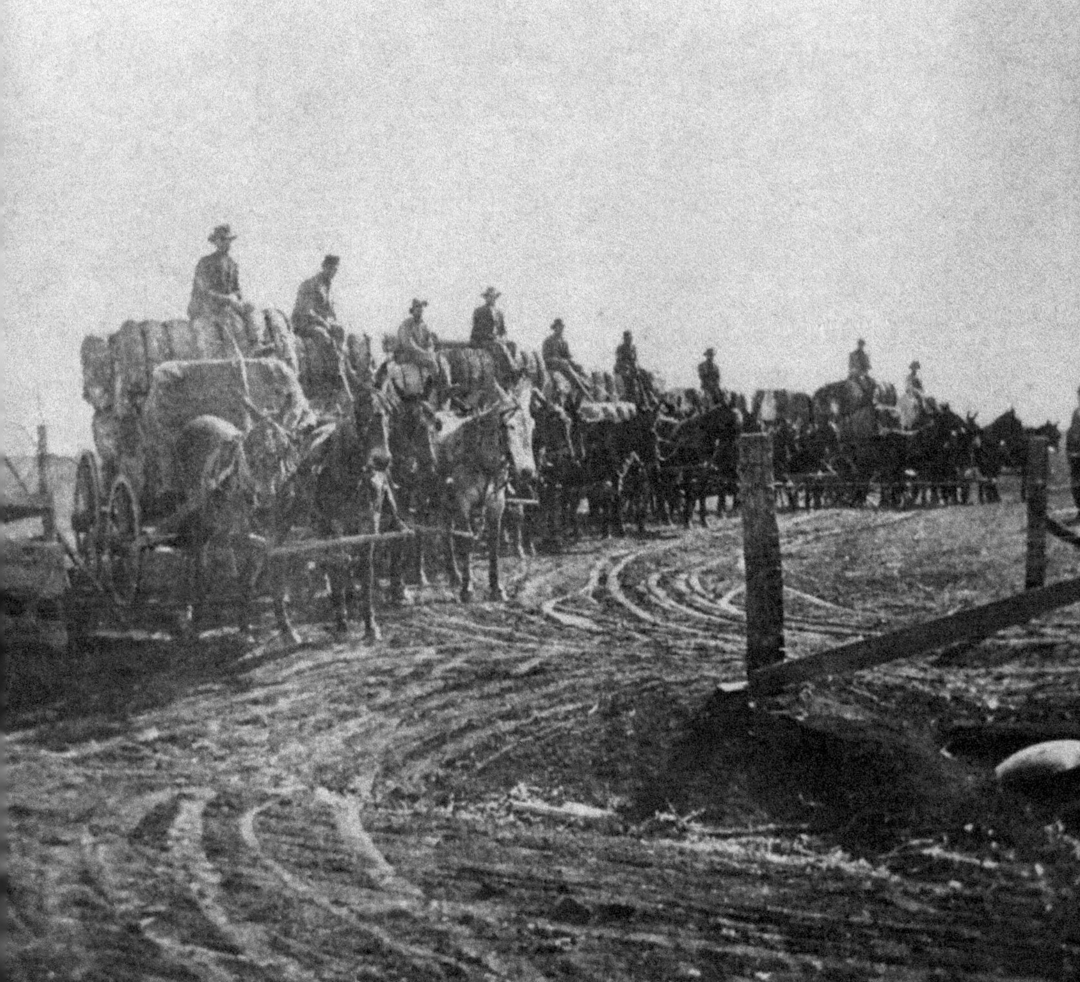

Cotton grown and harvested at the Rasor Farm was loaded onto wagons and taken to market in downtown Plano, as shown in this photograph dated sometime before 1900. The daylong expedition involved nine wagons driven by John Rasor's nine sons.

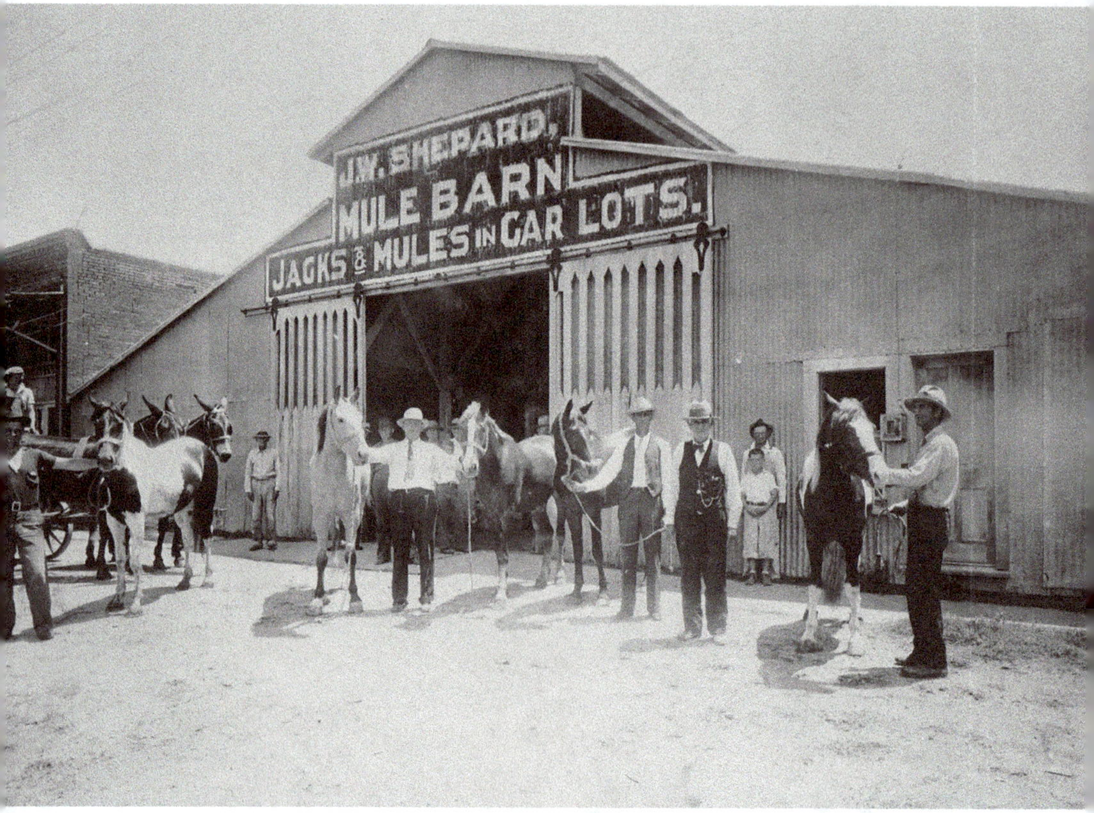

By the end of the Civil War, Plano had become the Mule Capital of the World. The business started with C.S. Haggard and a male donkey named Mammoth Jack, who sired the "Plano mules" known for their size, strength, and endurance. C.S.'s son-in-law John William "J.W." Shepard expanded the business with a mule barn near the H&TC depot, shown in the early 1900s. Today, a historical marker on the sidewalk just south of the Masonic Lodge notes the barn's former location.

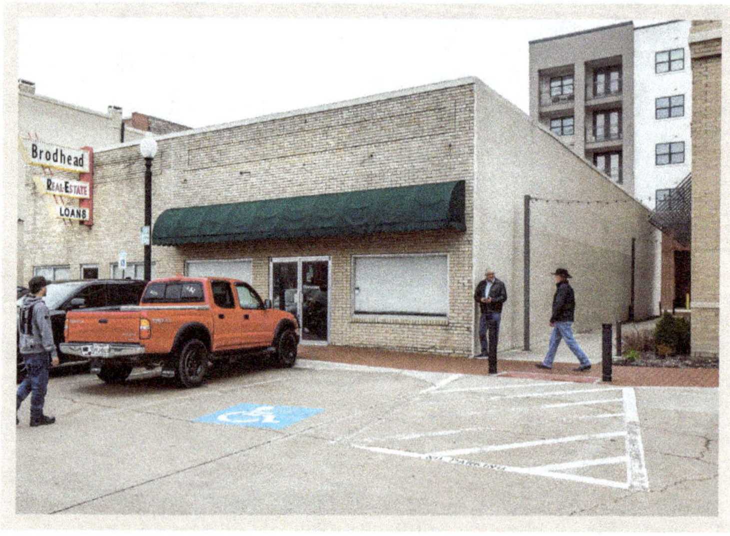

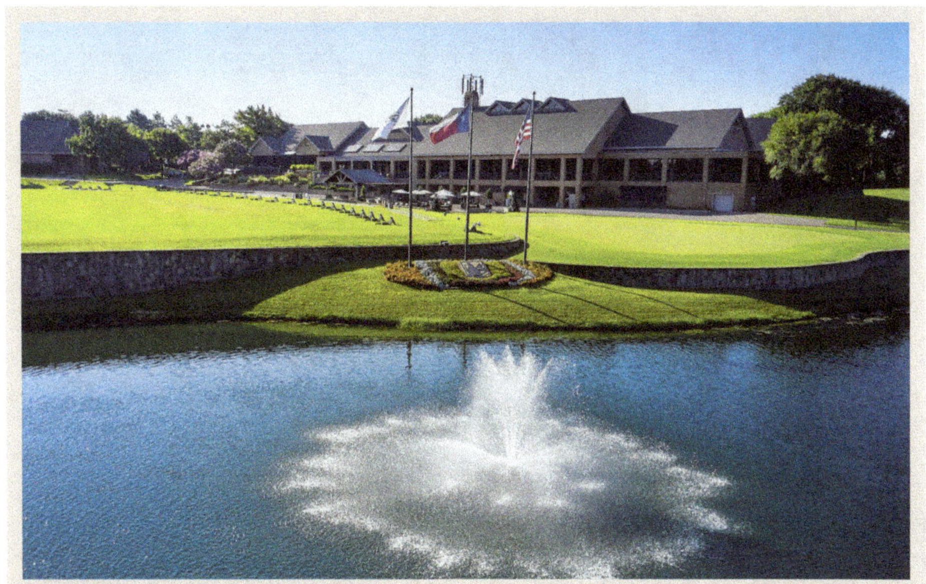

J.W. Shepard owned a 2,200-acre ranch and farm located where Gleneagles Country Club is now, on Park Boulevard near White Rock Creek in west Plano. Shepard, the namesake of Plano's Shepard Elementary School, was one of Plano's most prominent citizens. He owned 11 cotton gins and cottonseed oil and flour mills and served on the first Plano Independent School District (PISD) board and city council. Shepard died in 1946 at the age of 90. (Present, courtesy of Gleneagles Country Club.)

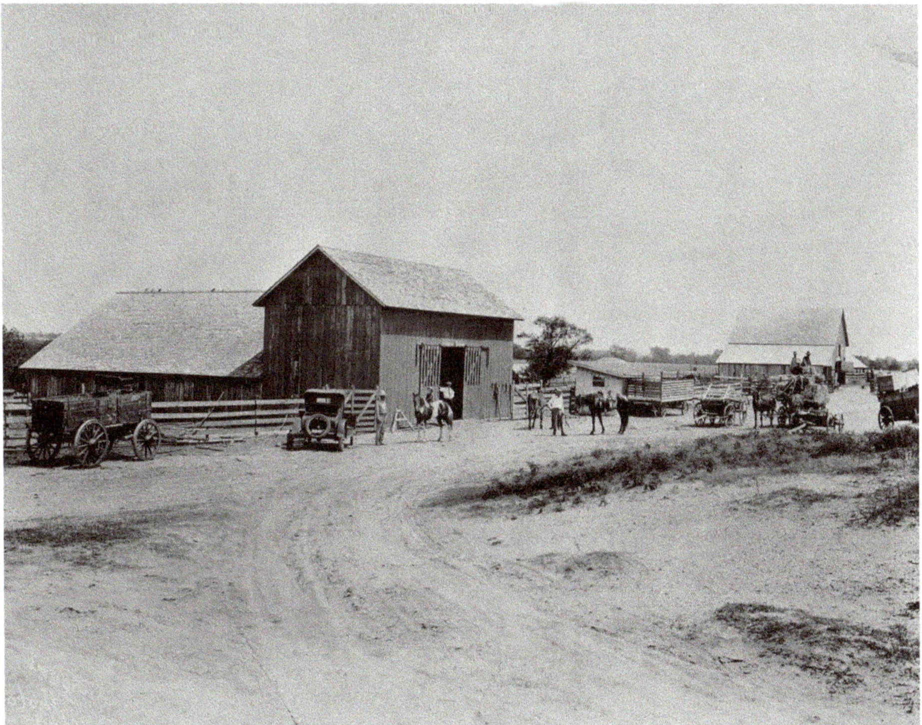

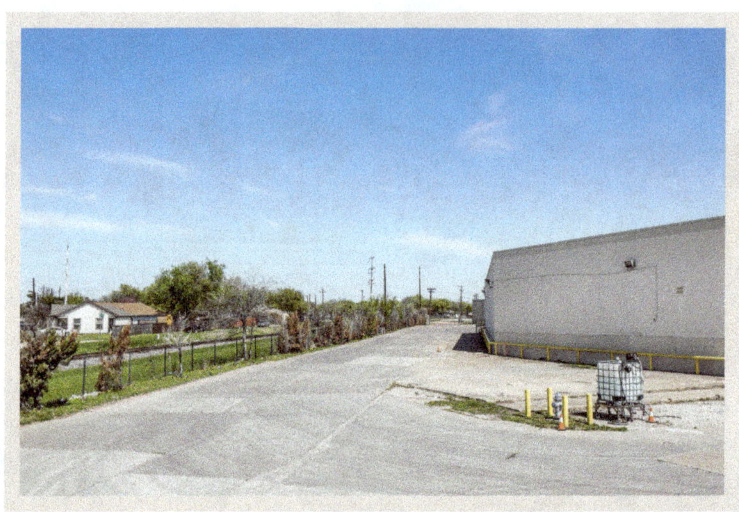

By 1900, cotton was king in Plano. In 1902, several businessmen organized the Cotton Oil Company to produce cottonseed oil, used primarily as fuel in lamps, machinery lubricant, and later in food preparation and soap production. The mill was strategically located near the Cotton Belt railroad tracks (today, the nearest address is 910 10th Street) to allow for easy shipping to markets in Arkansas, Missouri, and beyond.

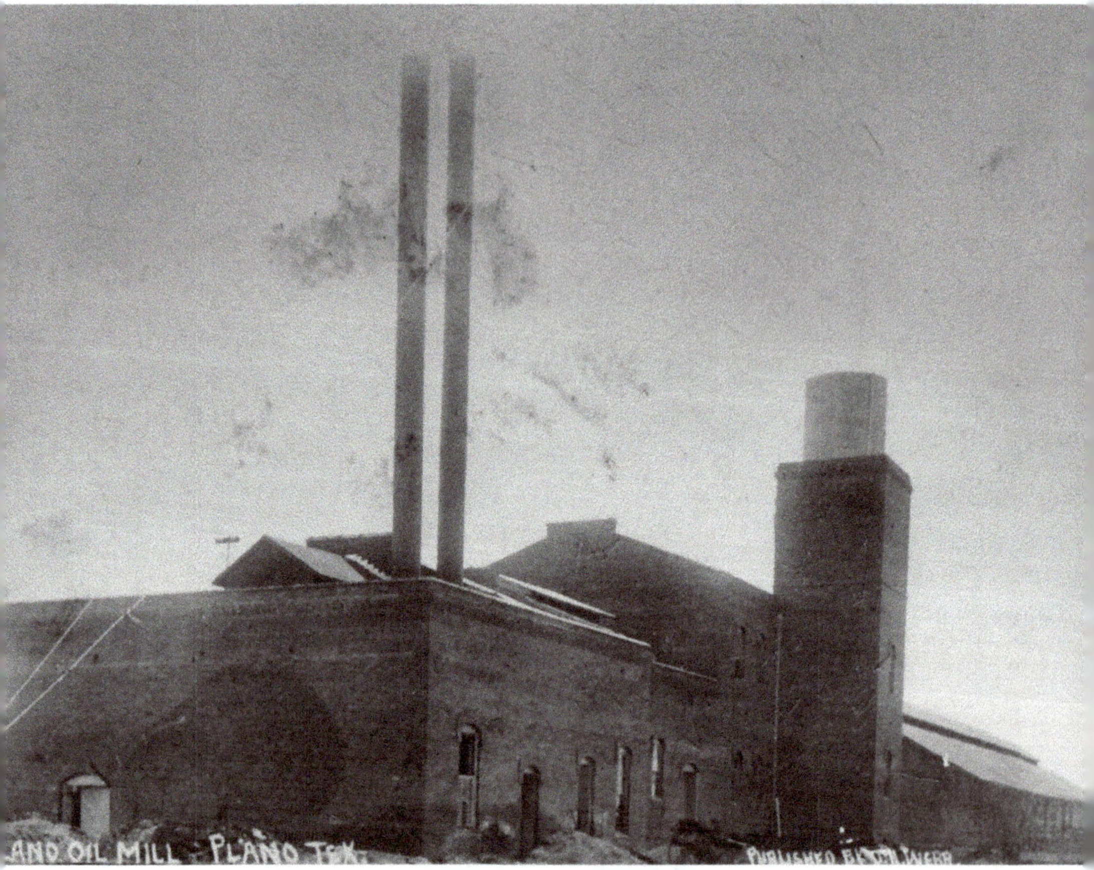

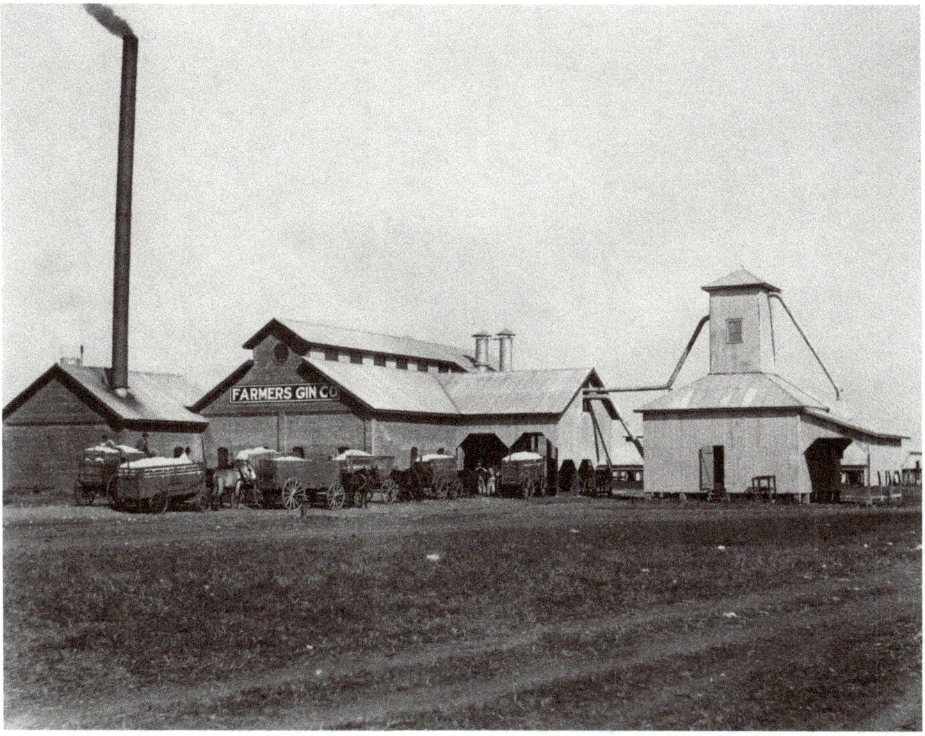

Four Plano citizens—J.H. Carpenter, Tom Andrews, Olney Davis, and R.A. Davis—formed the Farmers Gin Company in 1913. Wagons delivered cotton to the Farmers Gin, located on the south side of the Cotton Belt tracks, just east of where Municipal Avenue is today. The gin then shipped the ginned cotton on the Cotton Belt trains. Today, the Cotton Belt corridor is under construction for DART's new Silver Line light commuter rail connecting Plano to Dallas/Fort Worth (DFW) International Airport.

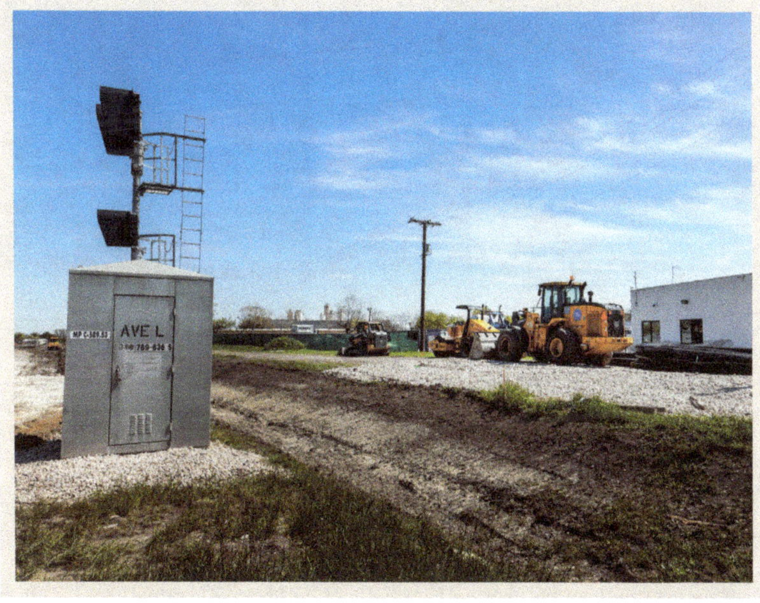

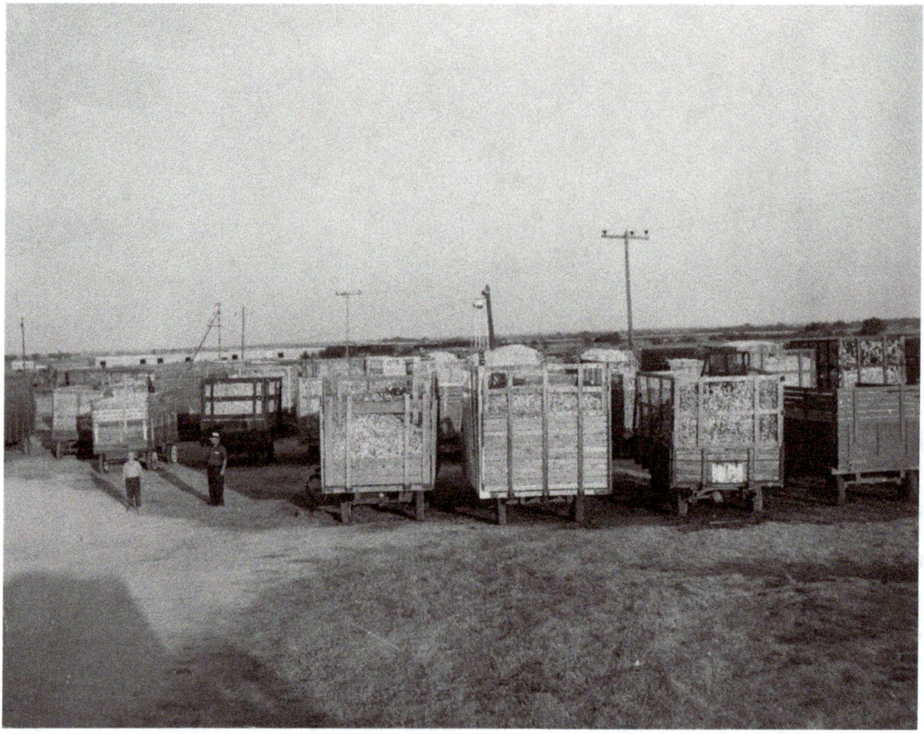

In 1938, seven Plano men formed a nonprofit cooperative for marketing and processing agricultural products under Texas's Cooperative Marketing Act. The Plano Cooperative Gin purchased the Huguley-Aldridge Gin that same year and the Farmers Gin of Plano in 1950. The operation dissolved in 1984, marking the end of Plano's 100-year cotton era. Today, the location (south side of the Cotton Belt rail line, east of K Avenue) is under construction for the 12th Street Station for DART's new Silver Line.

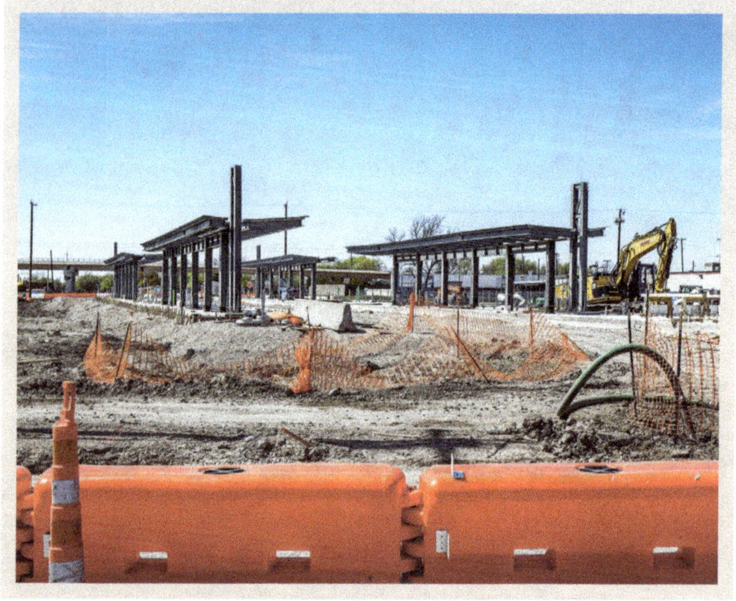

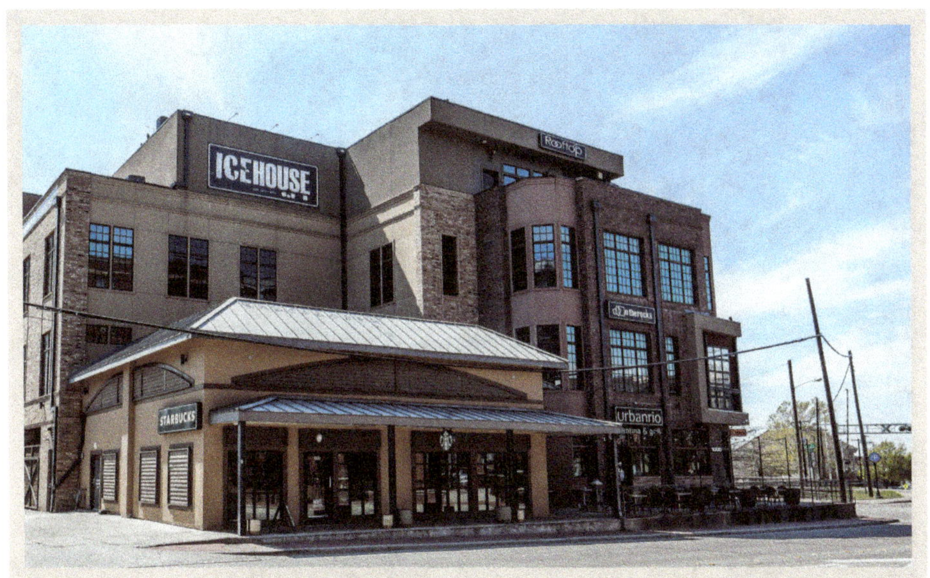


From the 1890s until the 1930s, several mills and ice plants occupied the south end of I Avenue, formerly known as Mill Street. The mills produced flour, bran, oats, and cornmeal; the ice plants manufactured ice for Plano residents' iceboxes and other refrigeration needs. Today, Urban Rio Cantina and Grill occupies one of those former icehouses at 14th Street and I Avenue.

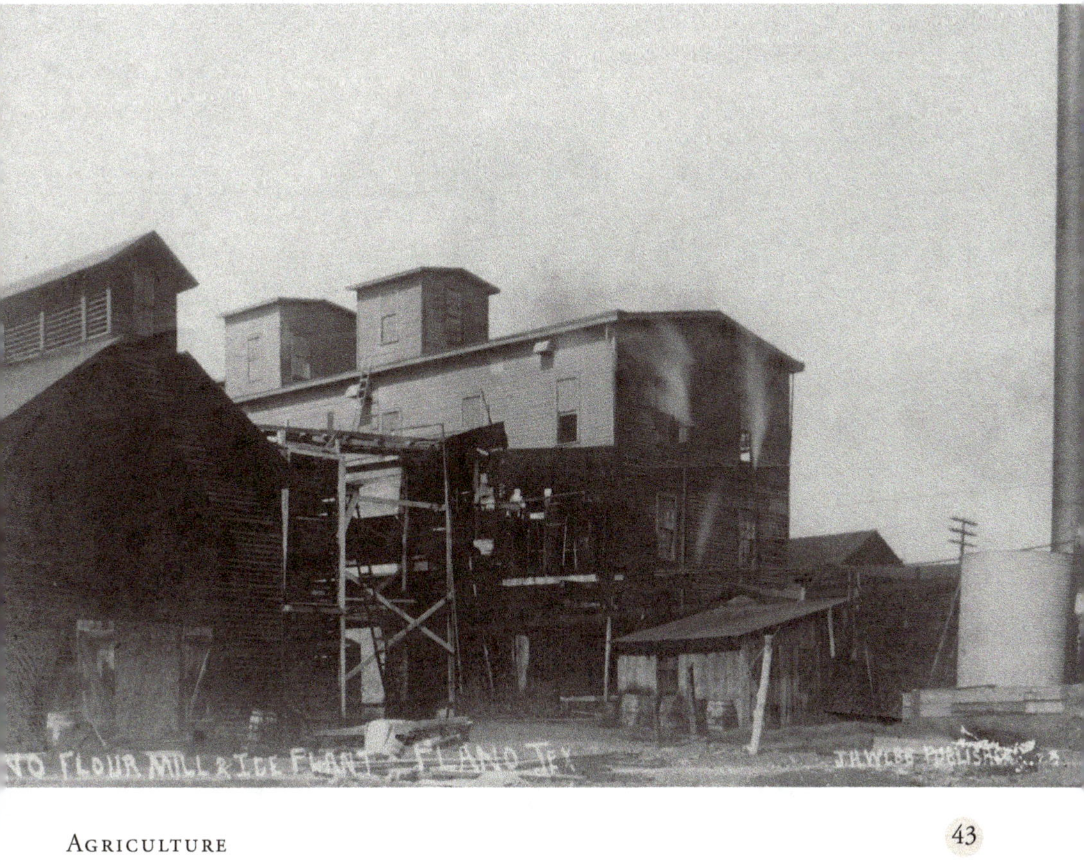

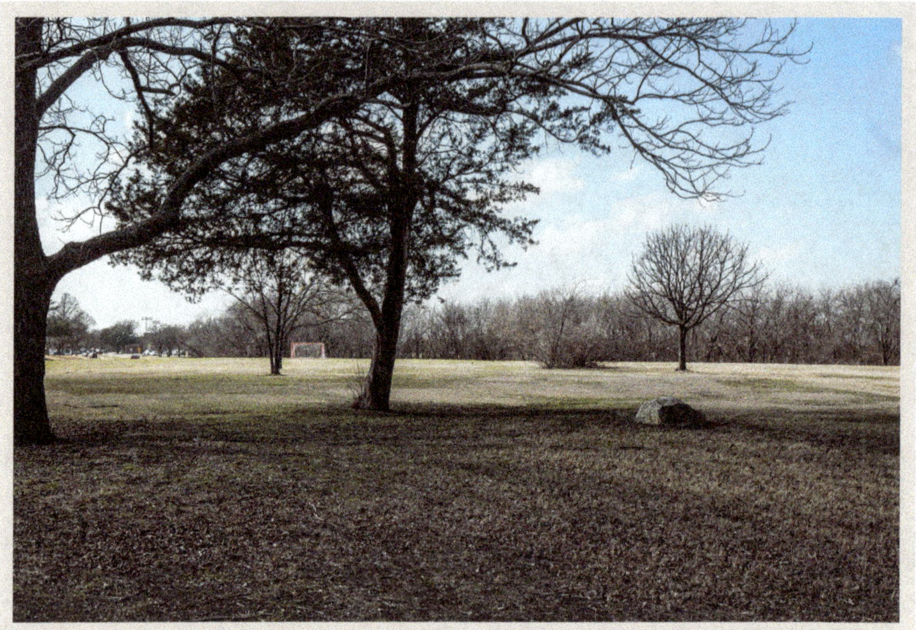

The John Rasor farm, pictured in about 1920, was located along what is now Russell Creek Drive and Independence Parkway. Today, a large rock marks the spot where the farmhouse likely once stood in what is now Russell Creek Park. Russell Creek is Plano's premier soccer park and the only park in North America with seven cricket fields in one location. In addition to a busy cricket league schedule, the park hosts at least one big-purse international cricket tournament each year.

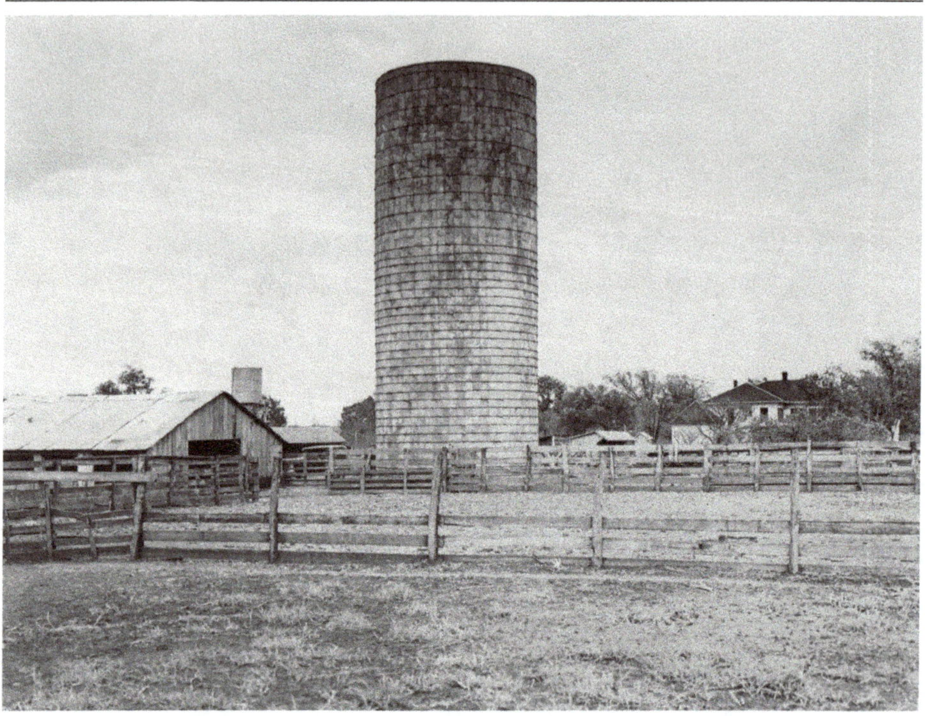

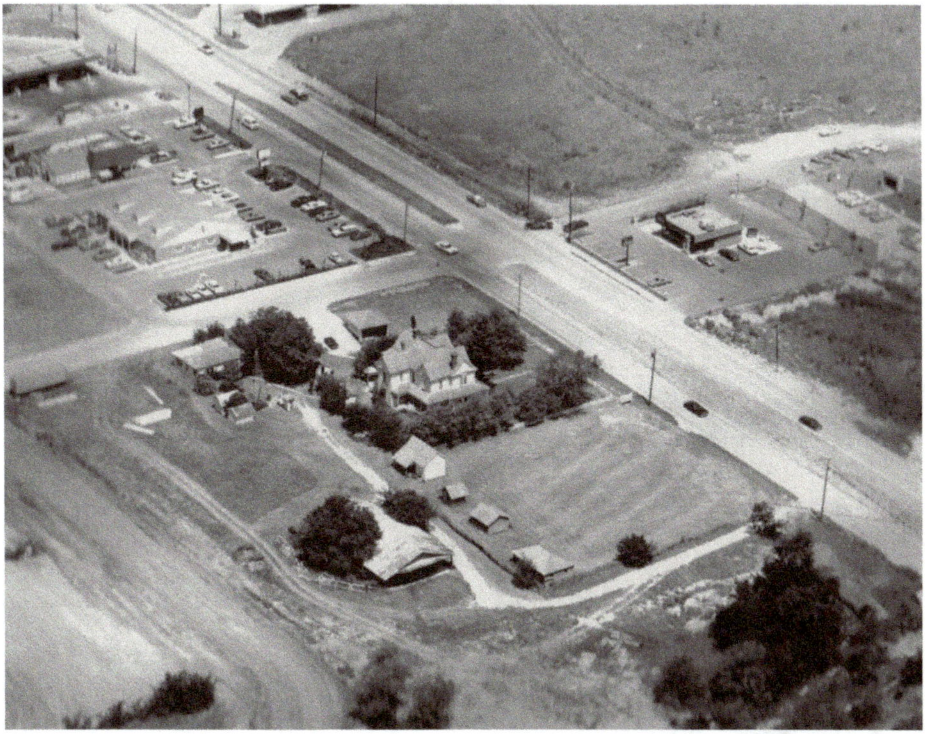

An aerial view, c. 1979, shows Ammie Wilson's house at 1900 West 15th Street. Built in 1891, the farm was originally 365 acres. Sheep dotted the pastures and cotton filled the fields. Today, the surrounding area is largely developed with homes and retail stores, but the house remains. Heritage Farmstead Museum keeps sheep and sponsors Future Farmers of America students interested in agricultural pursuits. The aerial photograph below was taken in 2023. (Past, courtesy of the Heritage Farmstead Museum; present, photograph by Jason Lavine.)

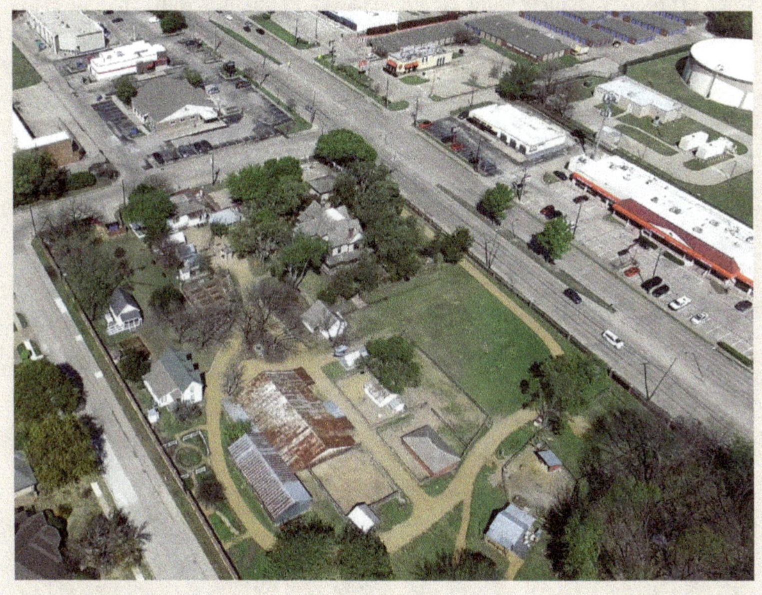

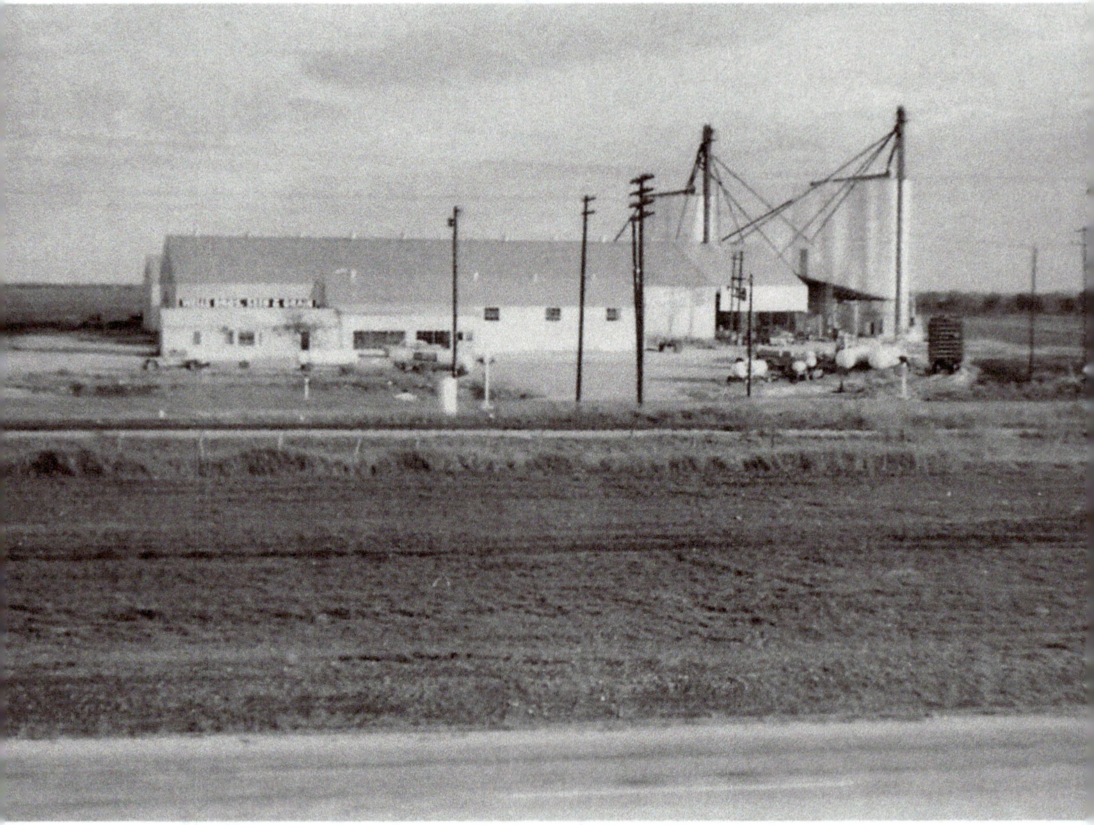

For more than 60 years, the Wells family has supplied Plano with an evolving selection of merchandise. The original Wells Brothers Seed Company, on what is now Coit Road, offered grain storage, tractors, and seed to farmers. Pictured above is the store in the 1960s, after it moved to Highway 5. Today, Wells Brothers Pet, Lawn and Garden Supply at 5001 K Avenue is still in the family and caters to organic gardeners and pet owners. (Past, courtesy of Nancy Wells Warder.)

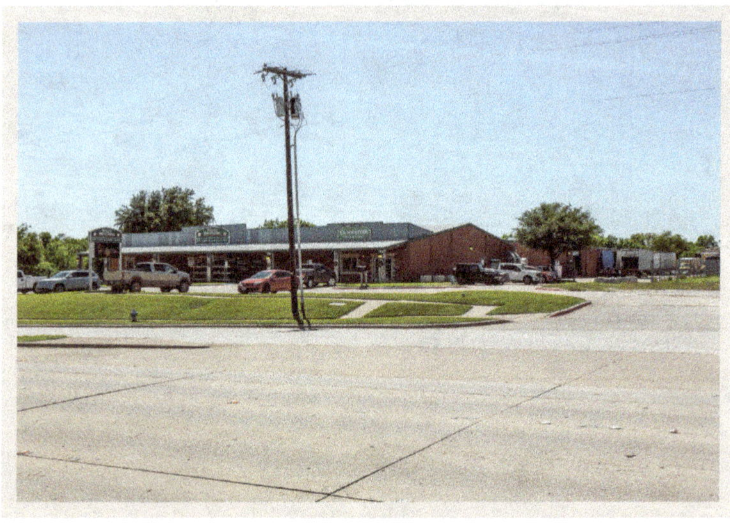

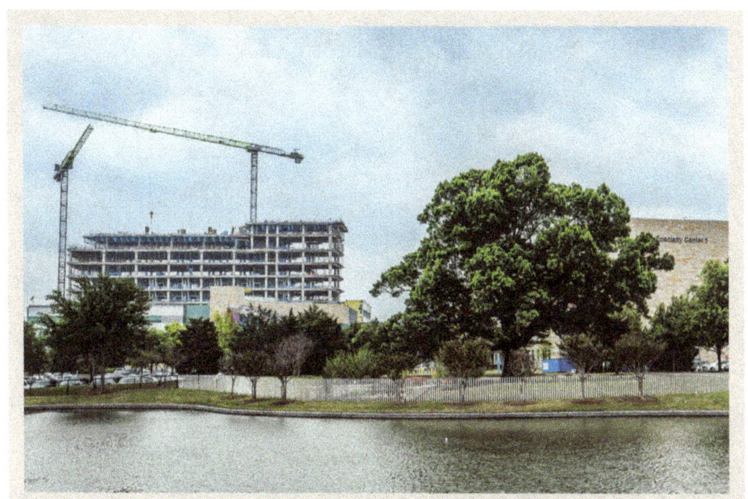

In the early 1980s, billionaire businessman Ross Perot Sr. drove around the farmland he had acquired in west Plano with Roy Wilshire, a project engineer, to map out the Legacy Business Park development. Perot often pointed out a large oak tree, imploring Wilshire to ensure the tree was never cut down. Today, the 100-year-old Story Tree still stands, a key landmark at Children's Medical Center Plano. The tree was likely there when the Haggard family, the first settlers, farmed the land. The ground-breaking photo below was taken in 2005 (Past, courtesy of Children's Health.)

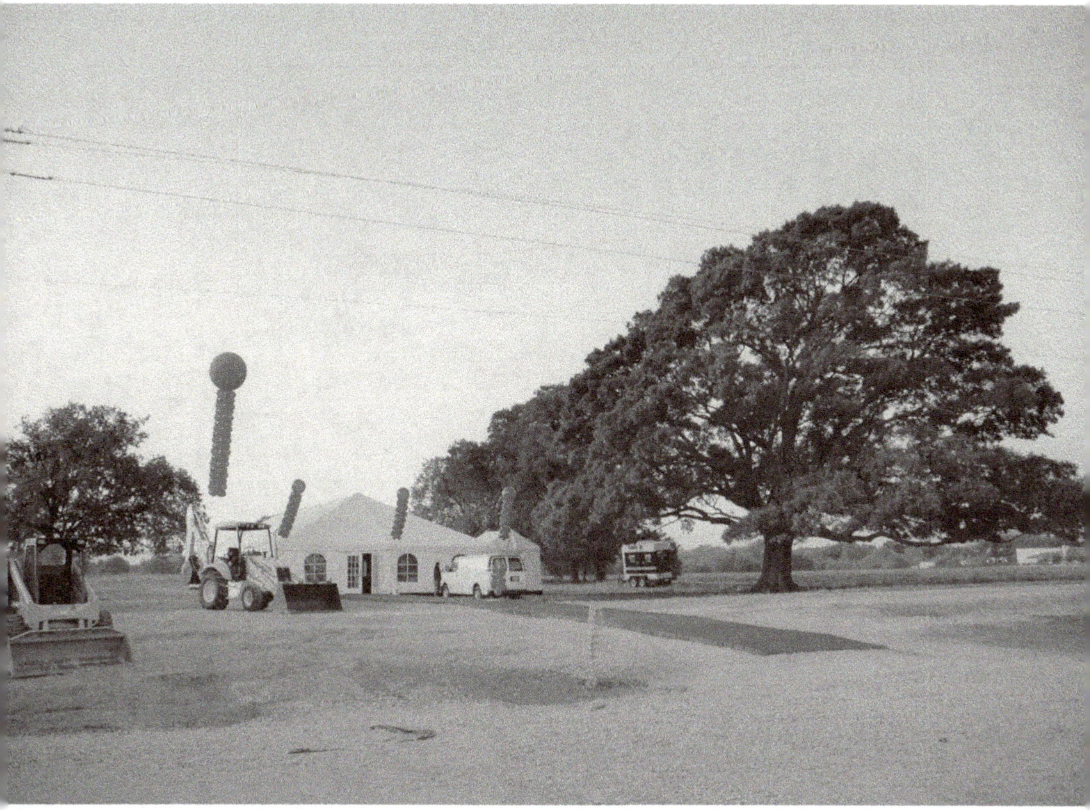

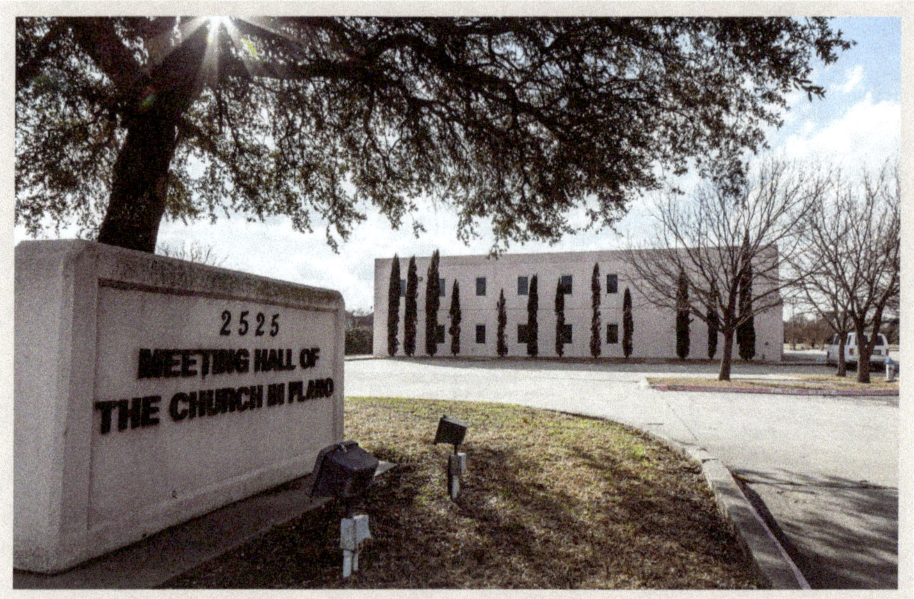


In the 1960s, Plano had its own pagoda, the centerpiece of the strange story of the University of Plano. The school for special needs students was the creation of New Jersey native Robert J. Morris. He convinced the Malaysian government to donate the 12,000-square-foot pagoda to the university; originally, the structure was Malaysia's pavilion at the 1964 World's Fair in New York. Financial issues forced the school's closure in 1976. Today, a church occupies the spot at 2525 Custer Road.

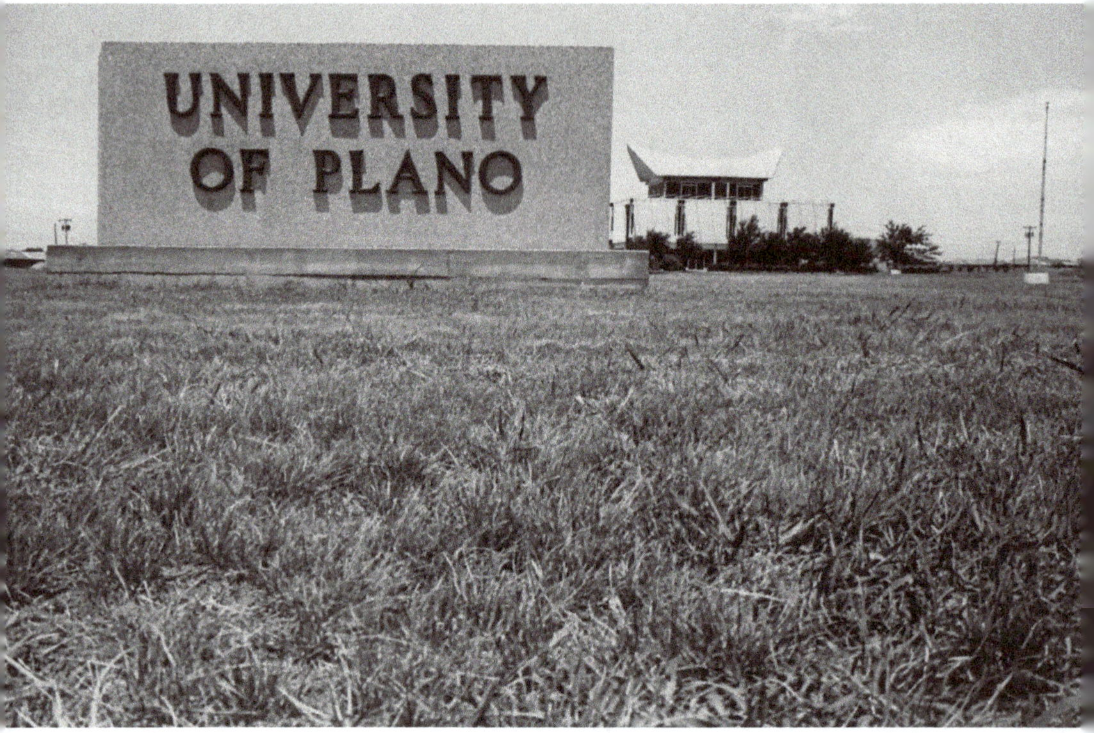

CHAPTER 4

# Community Life

## *Parades, Parks, and Police*

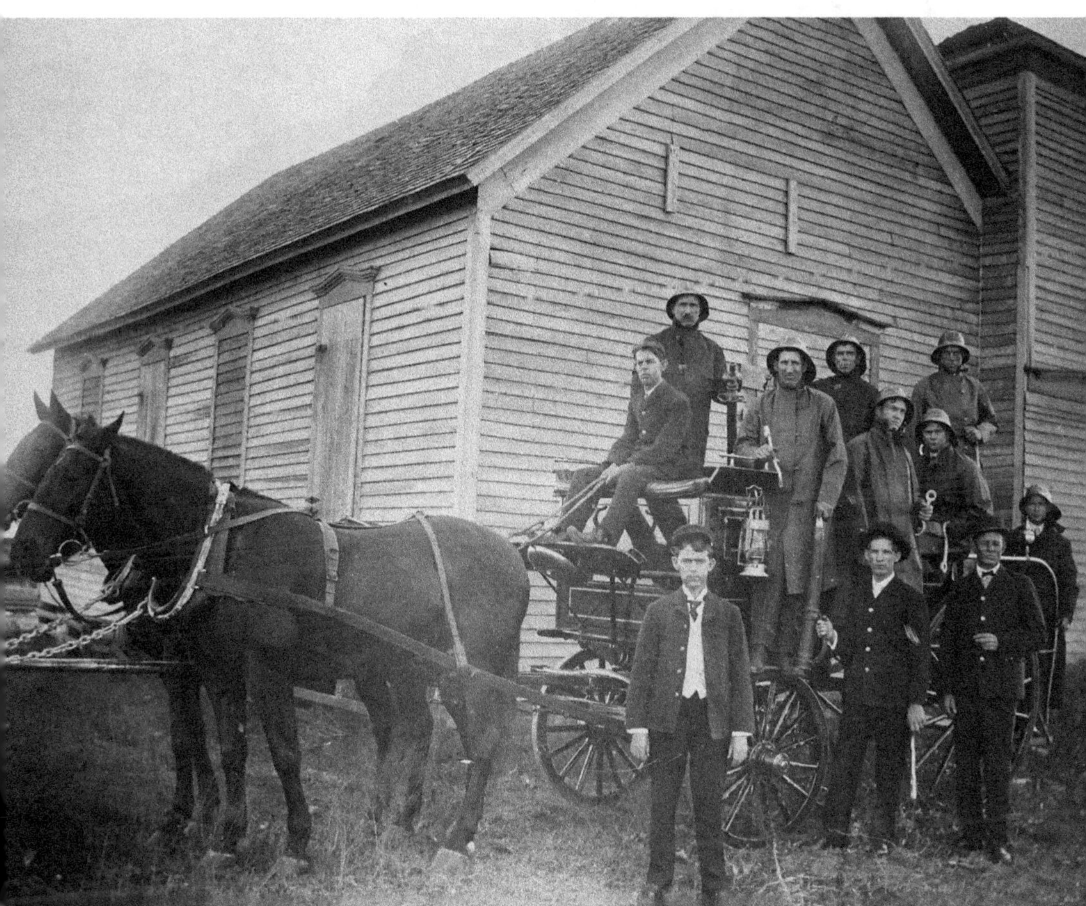

Firefighters pose in 1905 at the livery stable and station of the Plano Fire Department. Among those pictured are Dag Hudson (driving), Gee Hudson (front left), and Bob Howey (front row, far right.) Several devastating fires in the downtown area around 1895 led to the creation of Plano's fire department, now one of the best in the nation.

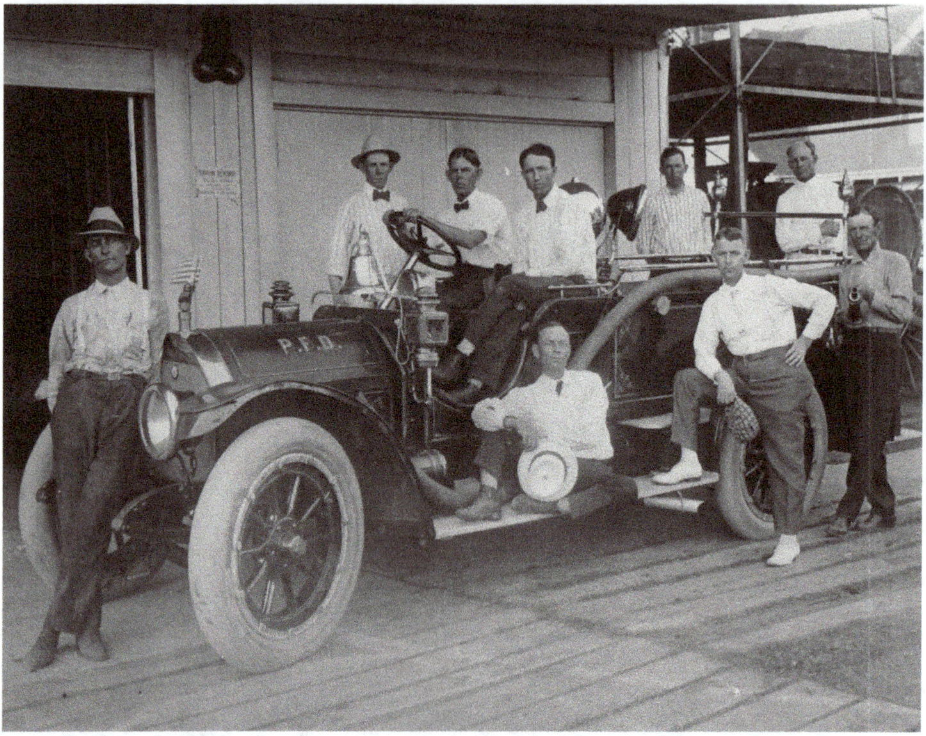

In the 1915 vintage photograph, firefighters stand with "Big Tom," Plano Fire Department's first automotive engine. In 2023, firefighters pose with a Quint 7 apparatus, which doubles as an engine and truck, at the new Plano Fire Training Center, which opened in 2022. Pictured from left to right are (first row) Lt. Daniel Daly, Capt. Matt Sutphin, driver/engineer Clayton Kemp, firefighter Raffi Kaftajian, driver/engineer Josh Ferrell, and firefighter Khyla South; (second row) firefighter/paramedics Josh Cates and Justin Nix.

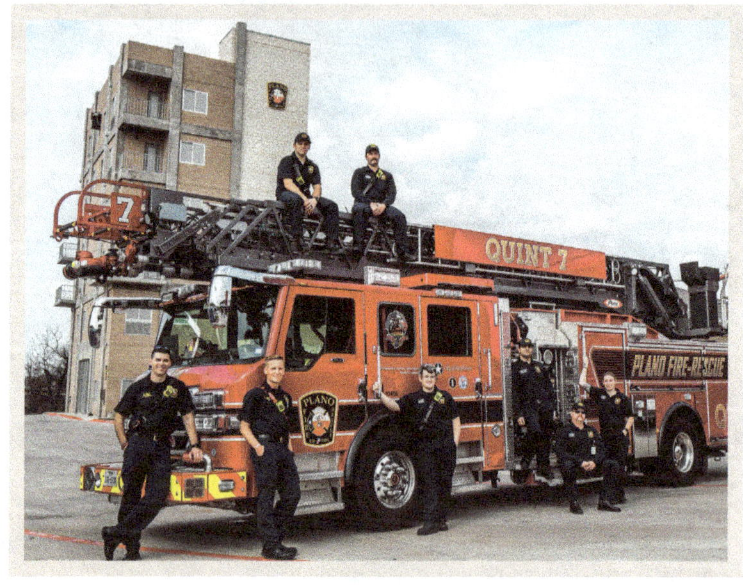

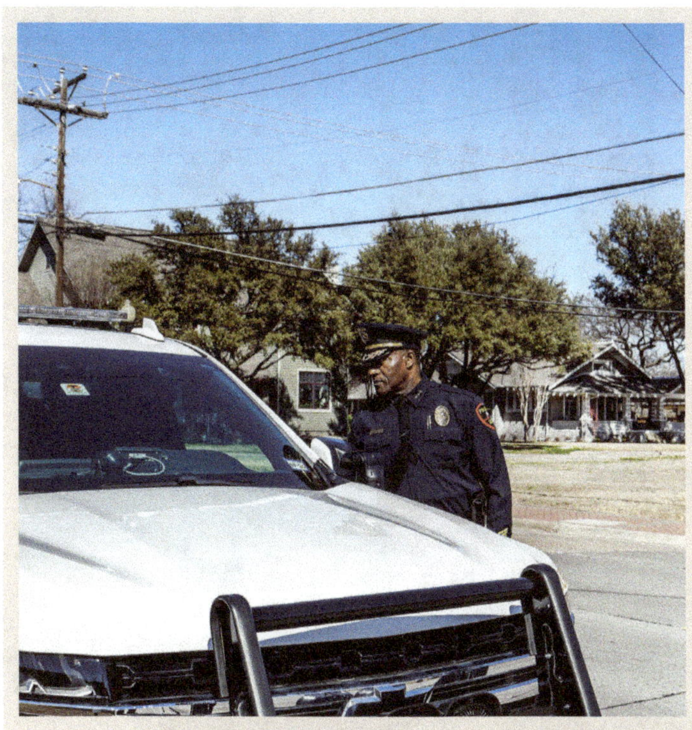

Chief of Police J.B. Toler, below, poses near his home at 16th Street and G Avenue. Toler was hired as the department's first sworn officer in 1959 and appointed chief in 1961. In 2023, Chief Ed Drain stands at the same spot. Drain was hired in Plano in 1994 and graduated through every rank in the department. After a stint as Amarillo's chief of police, Drain returned in 2020 to become Plano's first Black police chief.

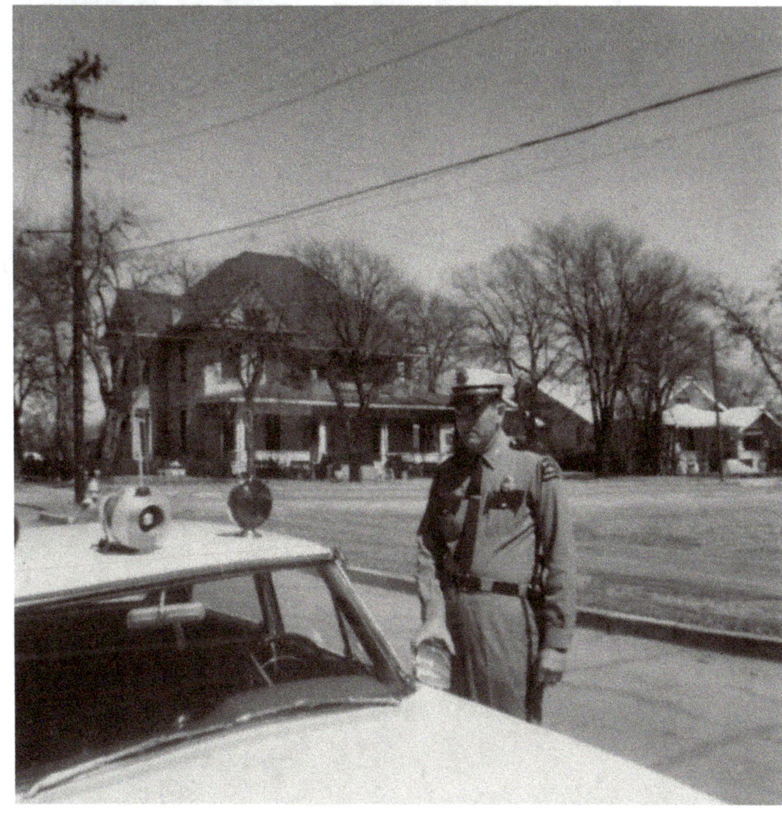

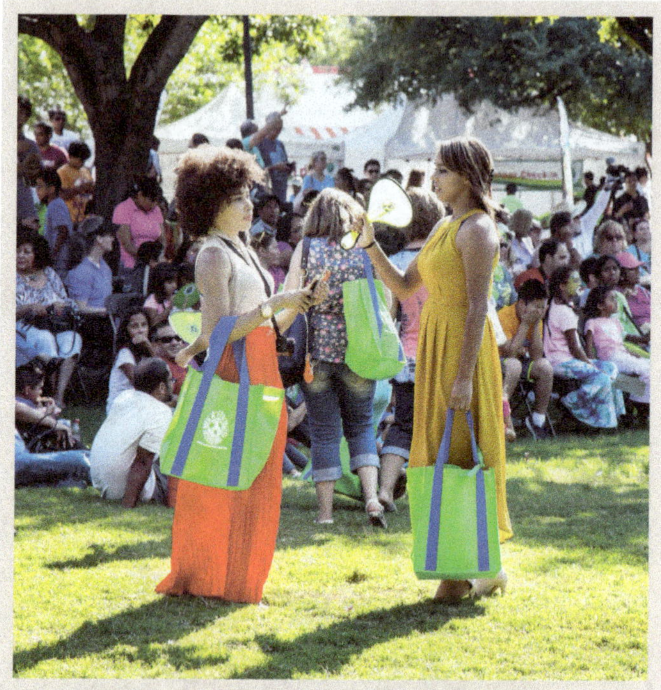

The Old Setters Picnic, honoring the city's pioneer families, was an annual highlight of community life in Plano from 1905 until 1934. The celebrations started with a parade through downtown ending at City Park, now Harrington Park. Today, thousands flock to numerous festivals held in Plano parks, including the International Festival, held in Haggard Park every October, pictured here in 2016.

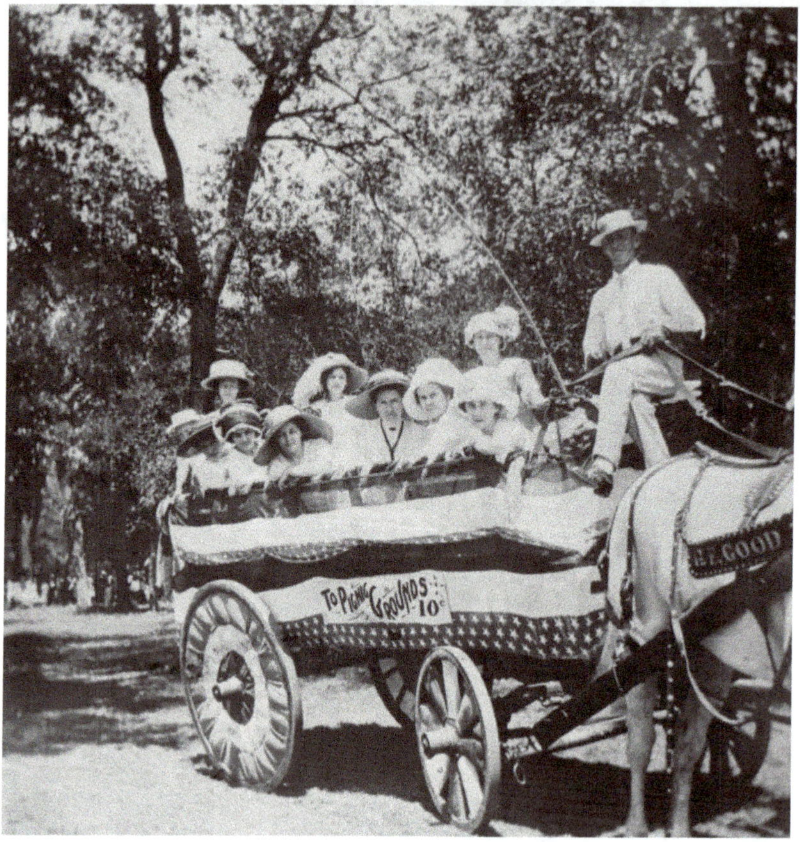

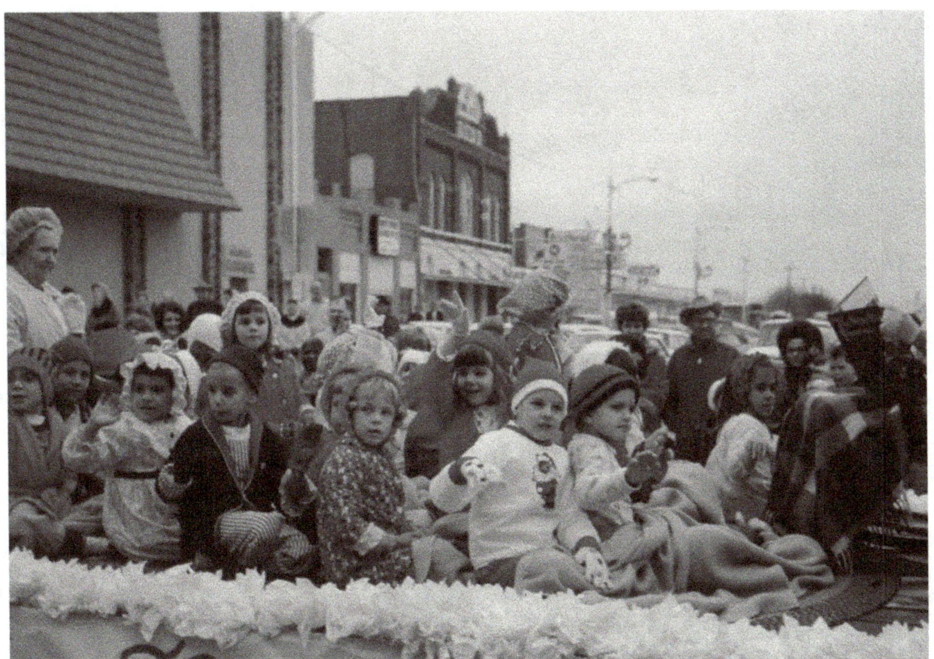

For many years, the Lions Club hosted the annual Christmas Parade through downtown Plano. Kids from the Happy Time Kindergarten enjoyed showing off their holiday pajamas in 1966. In 2019, girls and dads in the YMCA Adventure Guides program did the same. The Rotary Clubs of Plano will take over the Holiday Parade and Festival in 2023, after a three-year pause due to the COVID-19 pandemic and weather. (Past, photograph by Sam Smith, courtesy of Kemper Smith.)

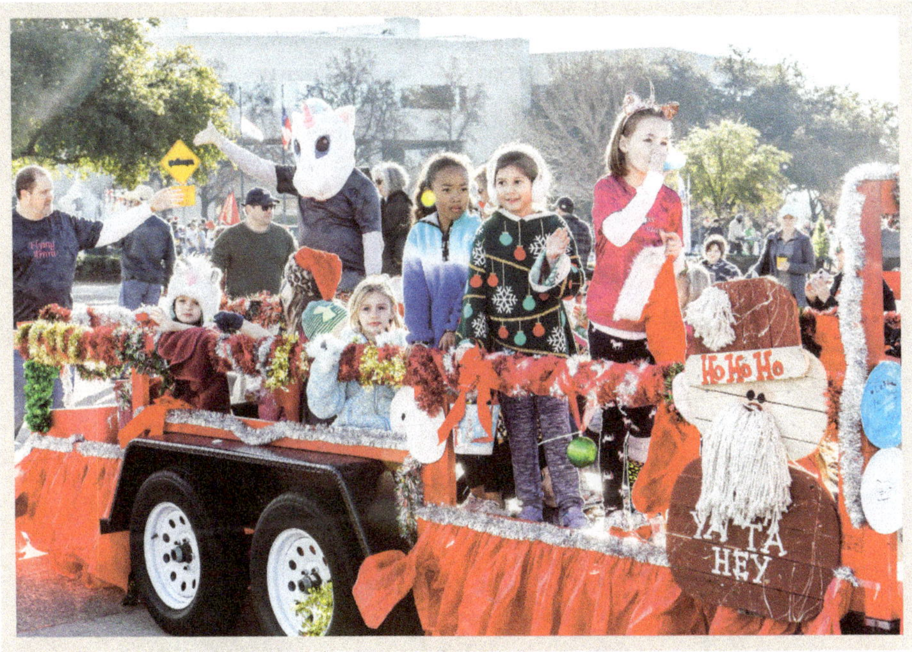

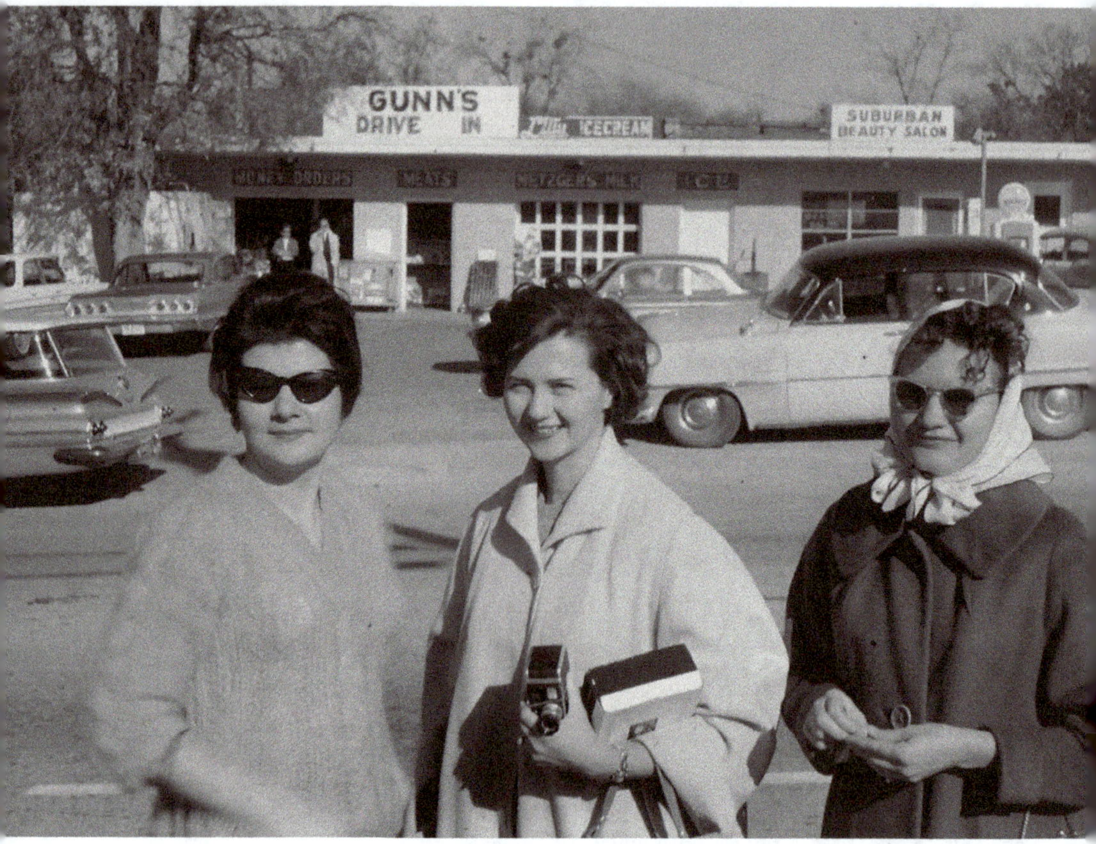

During the 1965 Christmas Parade, three Planoites pose in front of Gunn's Drive-in on 15th Street. From left to right are Margery Smith, Dot Forney, and Charlene Chronister. The city purchased Gunn's and other nearby land to expand Haggard Park in time for the Texas sesquicentennial in 1986. In 2023, Plano East graduates and sisters, from left to right, Susana Marks, Elisa Klein, and Roció Gosewehr Hernández enjoy the park. (Past, photograph by Sam Smith, courtesy of Kemper Smith.)

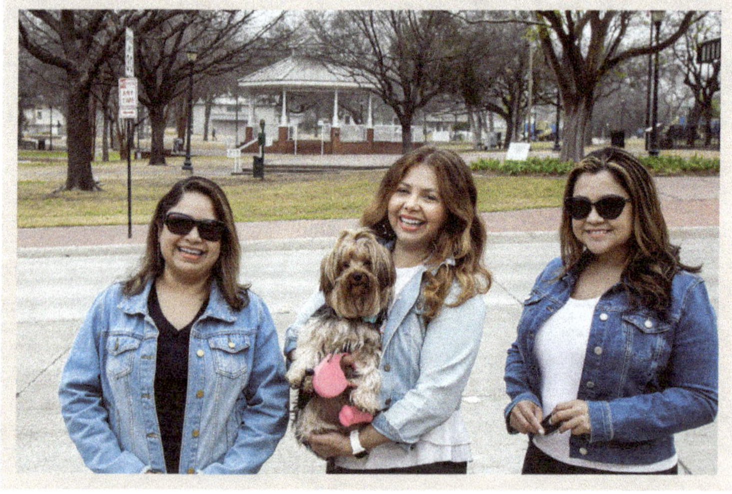

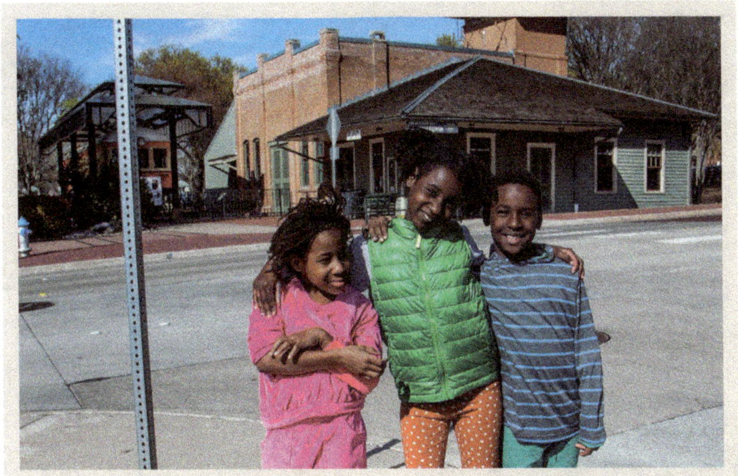

Children were raised "free range" at the time of this c. late 1940s photograph below. The three unidentified young Planoites were roughhousing near the Interurban Railway station, which was closed by that time. However, having fun never gets old. Pictured in 2023 are siblings and Plano students, from left to right, Stokely, Sloane, and Miles Cook in front of the Interurban Railway Museum. (Past, courtesy of the Plano Conservancy Collection. )

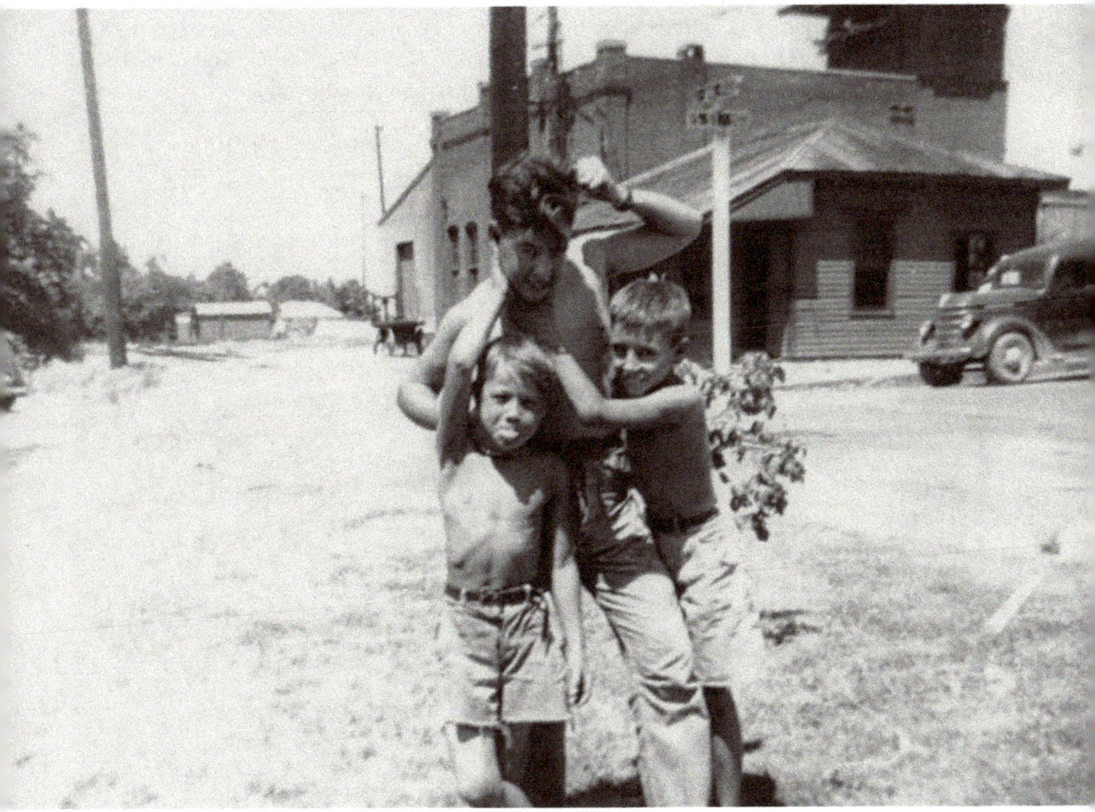

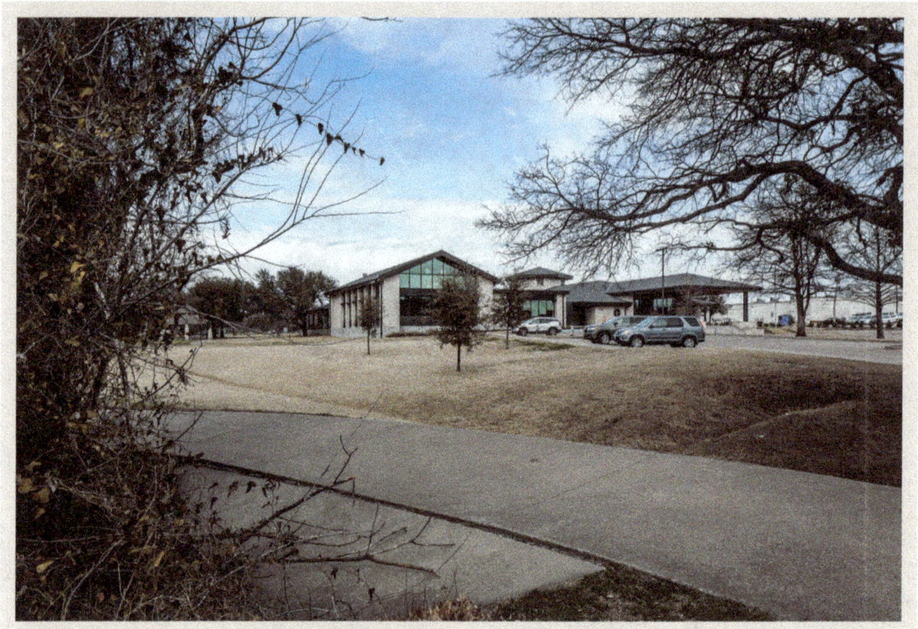

By the late 19th century, the city of Plano began adding infrastructure to support its growing population, including telephone (1883), water (1897), and trash and sewer service (1909). This photograph shows the city's waterworks in 1910, located at Spring Creek near 16th Street. Today, the area is part of Harrington Park and home to the Sam Johnson Recreation Center. Traces of the old water system are still visible.

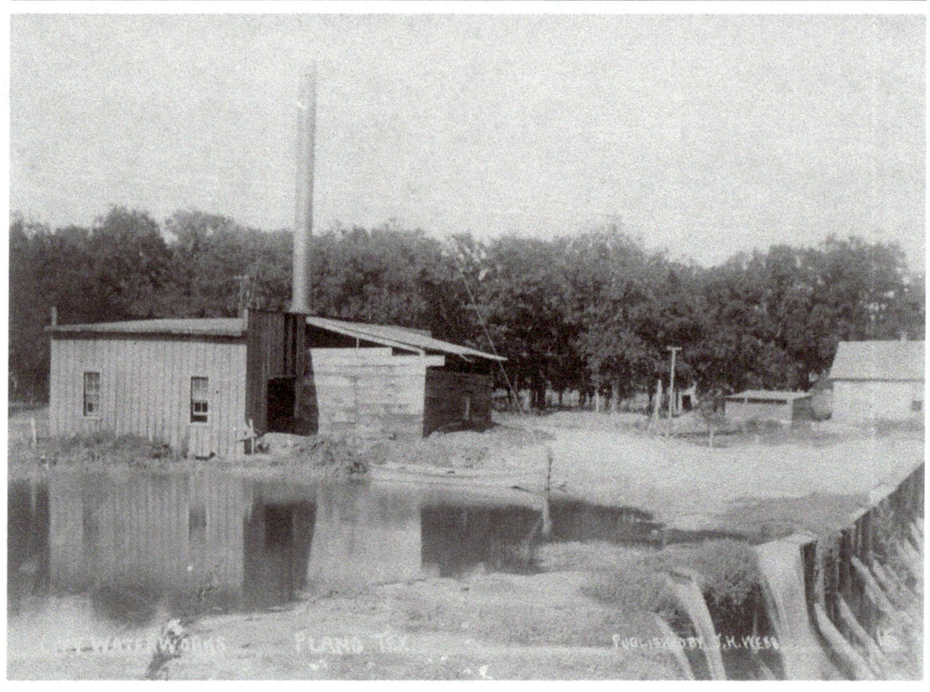

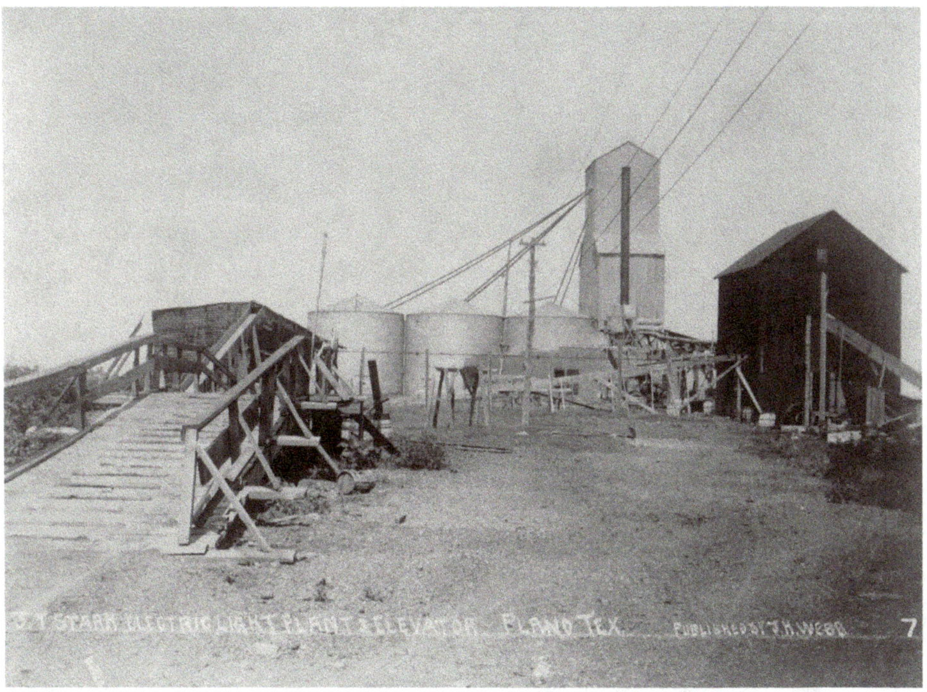


Electricity arrived in Plano in 1899 when J.T. Stark (1864–1923) built the Electric Light Plant & Elevator, located near the Cotton Belt rail line and what is now Municipal Avenue. Electric lights arrived in New York City and Dallas around 1882, but much of rural Texas had no electricity until the Rural Electrification Act of 1936 provided federal loans to install electrical distribution systems in isolated rural areas of the United States.

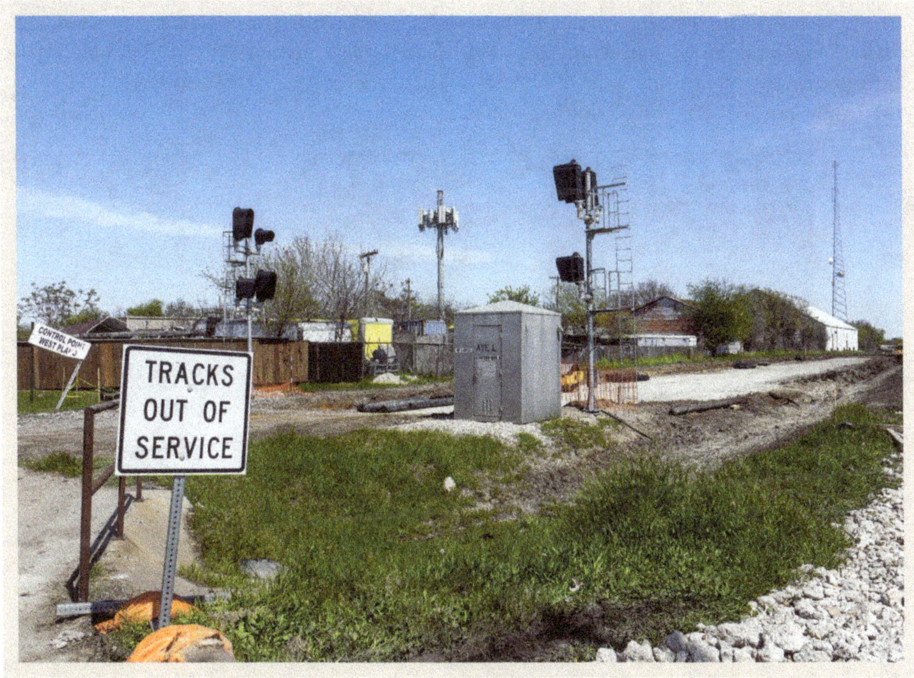

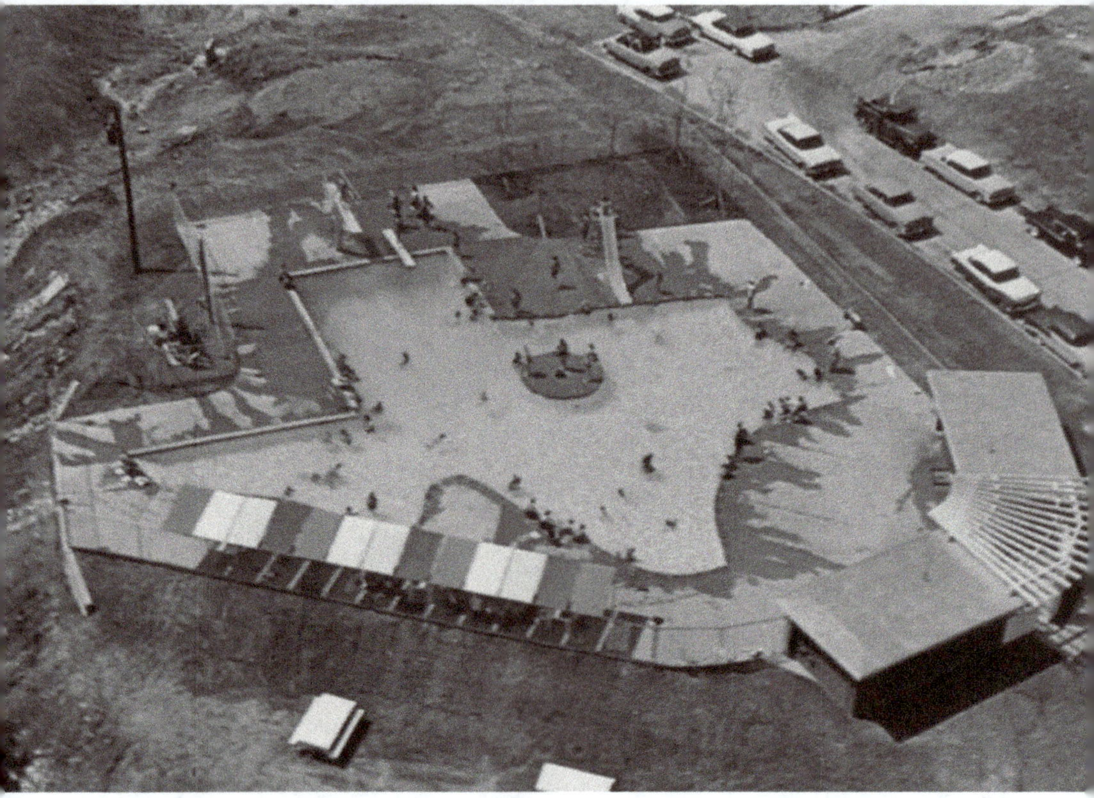

Possibly the oldest existing Texas-shaped pool, the Texas Pool was built in the early 1960s as part of Dallas North Estates, one of Plano's earliest large residential developments, by Hunt Properties, owned by one of Texas's most iconic families. By 2007, the pool was in danger of closing. Residents teamed up to renovate the pool and obtained a National Register of Historic Places designation. The pool is located at 901 Springbrook Drive. (Both, courtesy of the Texas Pool.)

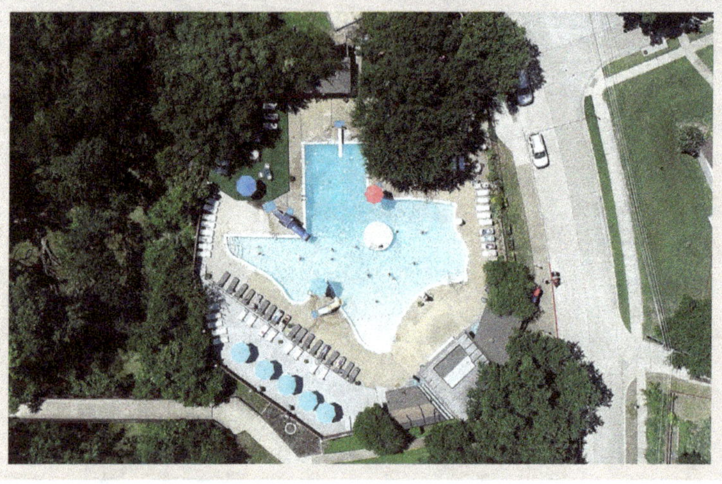

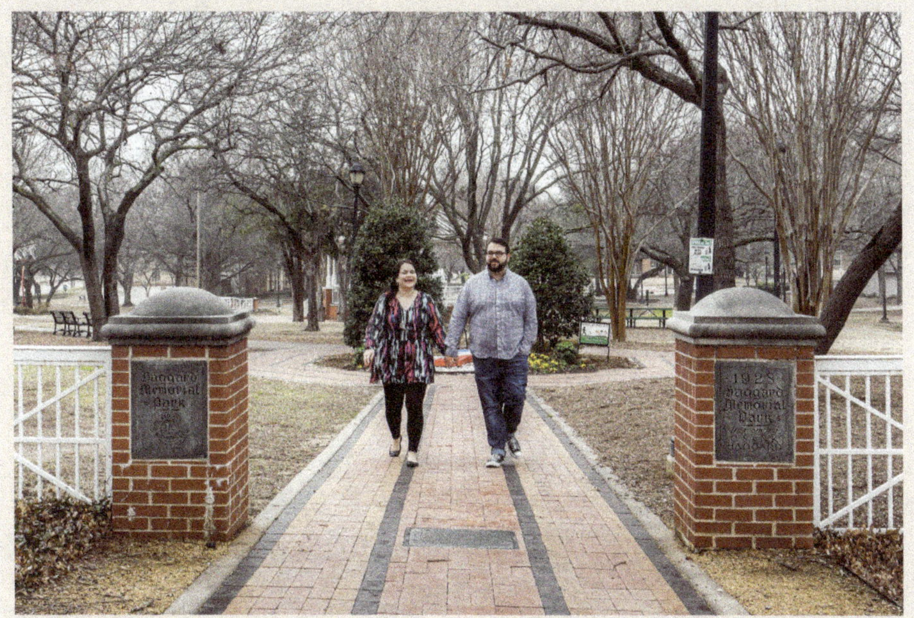


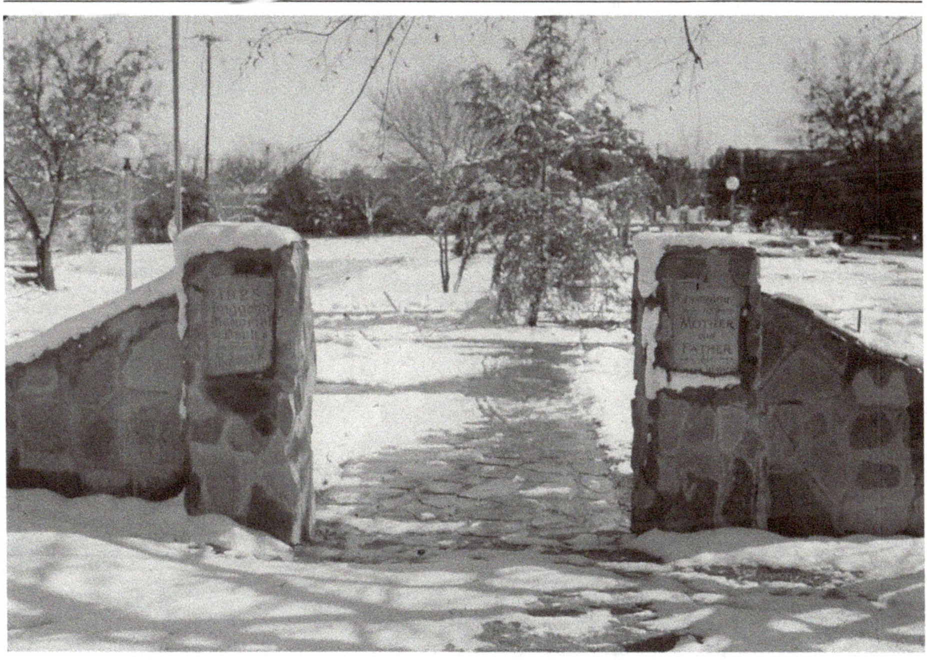


These entrance posts to Haggard Park originally stood elsewhere but were moved to the east entrance when the park was expanded in 1986. Opened in 1928, Haggard Park was once confined to a small area surrounding the pond, but the city purchased land for expansion over the years. Today, visitors like Emmy Lou Harris and fiancé Phil Lucia come to the park to enjoy the pond, gazebo, and playground. (Past, courtesy of Plano Parks and Recreation Department.)

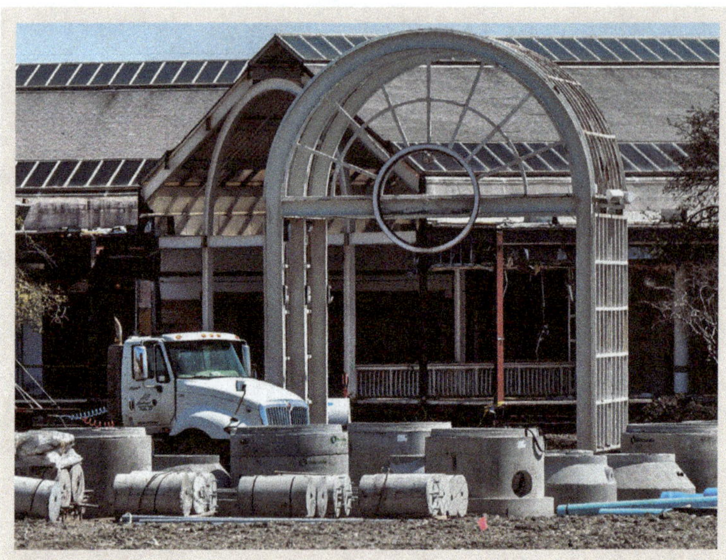

The arched canopy entrances were among Collin Creek Mall's most distinctive features when the mall opened in 1981. In 1990, Design Response added color and images of creek fauna (like the butterfly, pictured) to help shoppers remember where they had parked. Redevelopment began in 2019. When it opens, Collin Creek will feature housing, office, and retail space. Little of the old mall will remain, but the iconic canopy will stay. (Past, courtesy of Andrew Shell.)

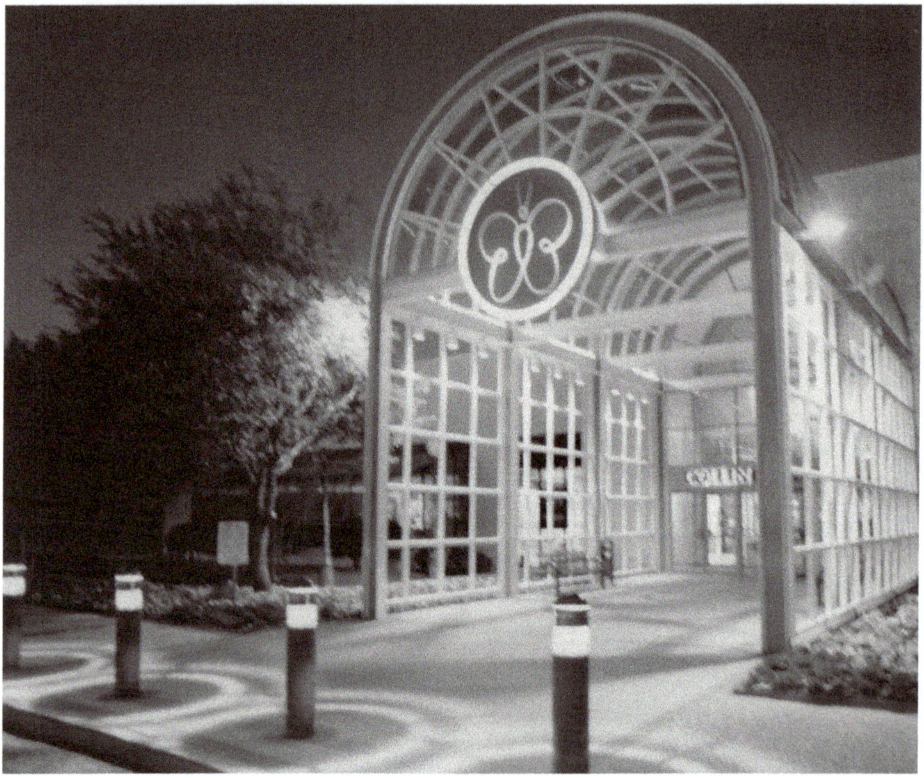

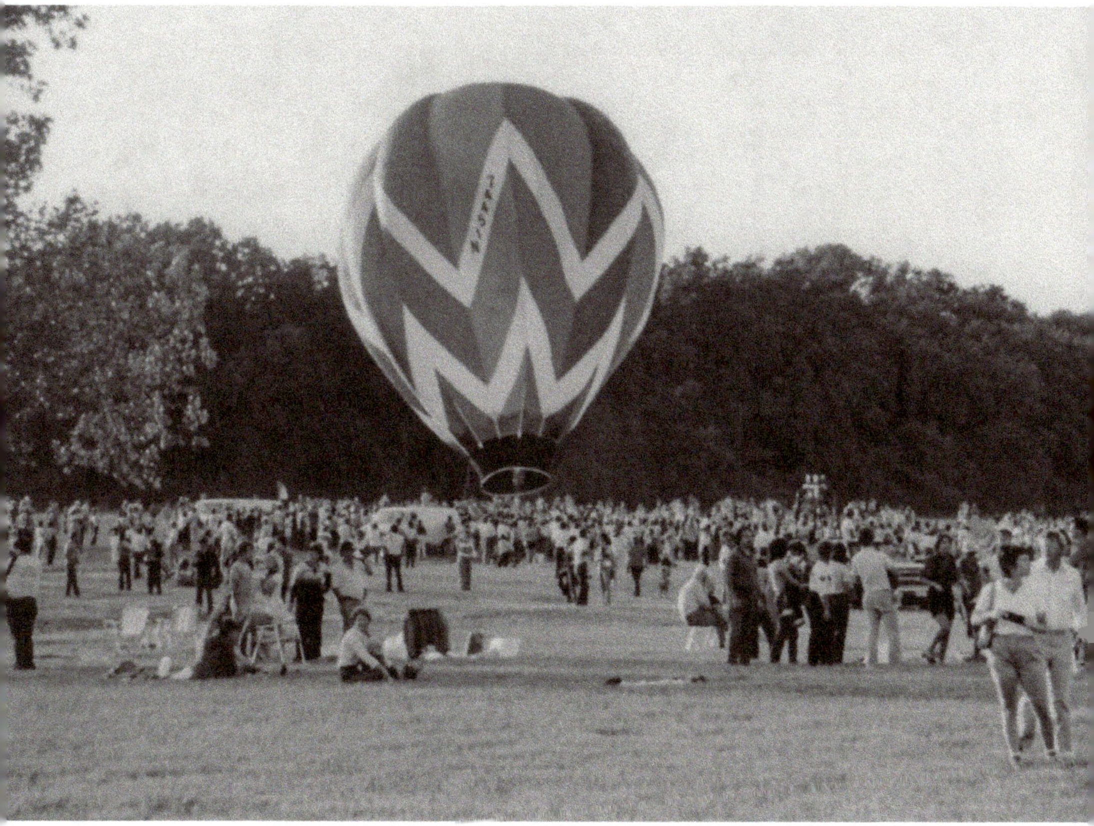

In 1983, the Plano Balloon Festival took place at what is now Bob Woodruff Park. Starting with the first Plano Balloon Rally in 1980, the event made Plano "the Balloon Capital of Texas." The 2023 festival at Oak Point Park and Nature Reserve will mark 42 years of ballooning in Plano. The 1983 image is courtesy of Don Wendell, who was with Plano's Parks and Recreation for 28 years, serving 23 years as director until retiring in 2009.

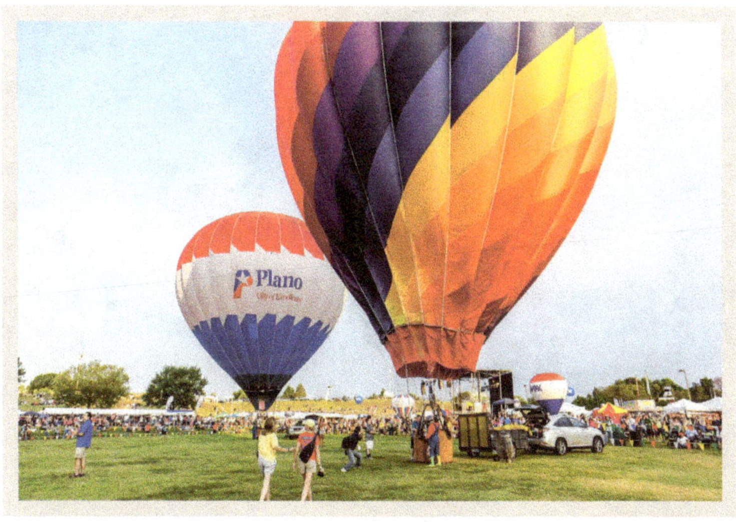

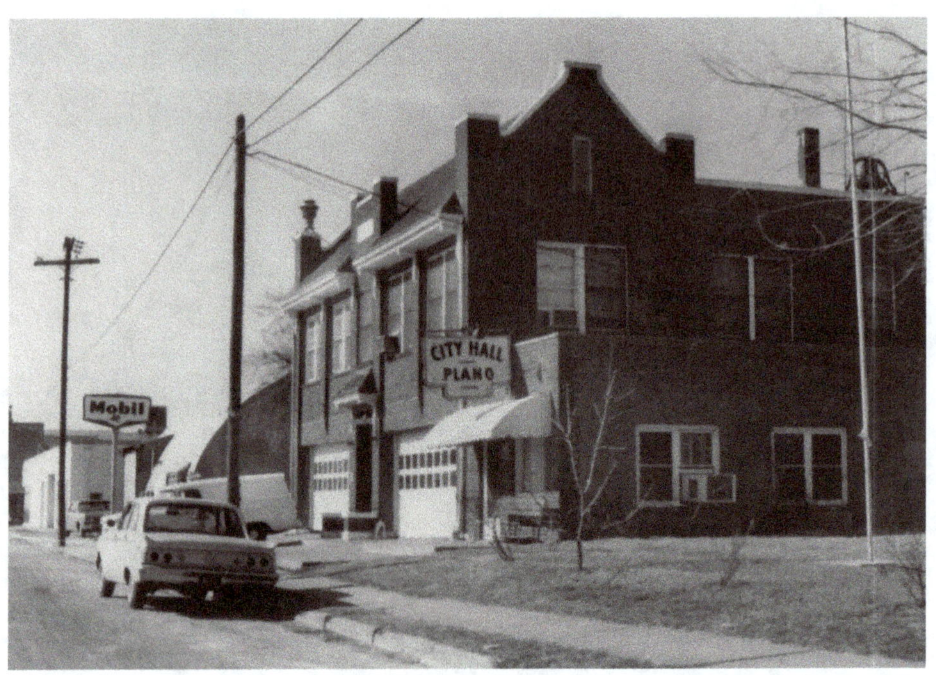


Built in 1923, Old City Hall was home to municipal offices, the police department, and the fire station for about 50 years. The redbrick building had fire truck bays flanking the entrance and offices upstairs. The current Plano Municipal Center, located nearby at K and Municipal Avenues, was built in 1980 and expanded in 1991. Pictured near Old City Hall's former location is Frank Turner, who served on the city staff for 32 years, retiring as deputy city manager in 2016.

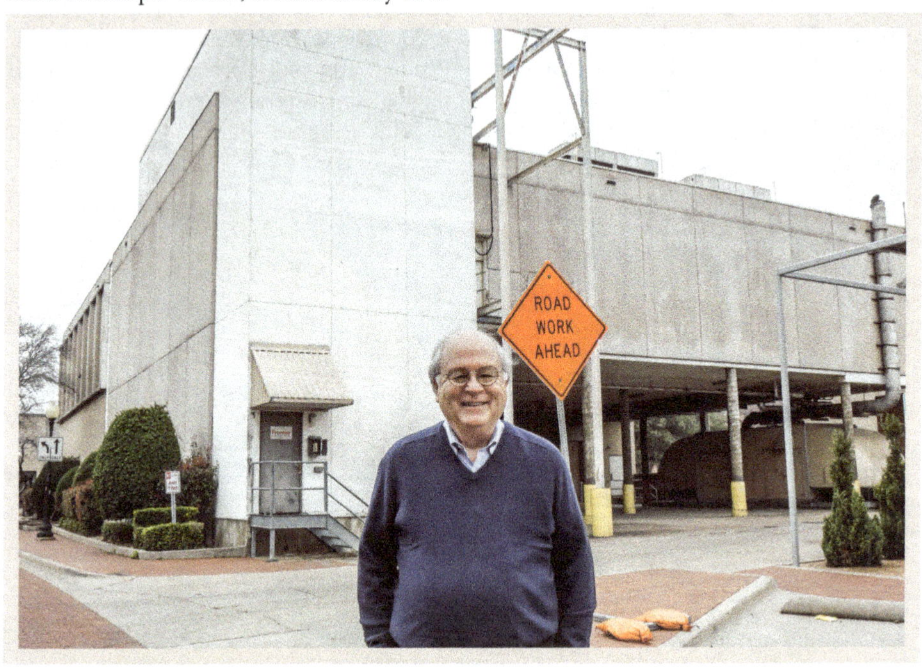

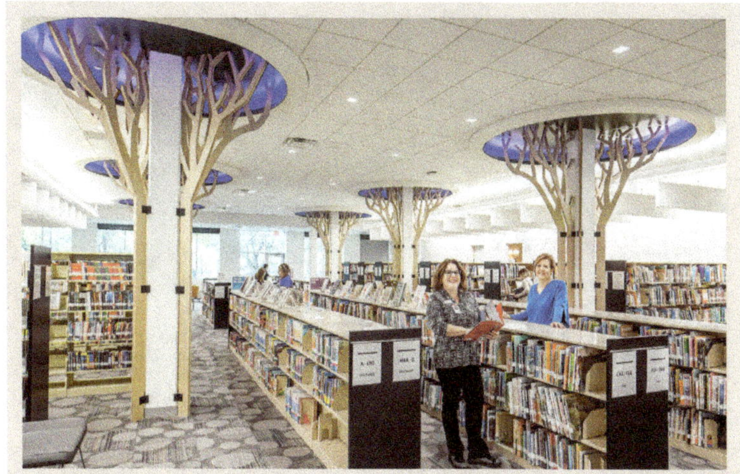

Plano built its first municipal library in 1969 at 1501 18th Street. The 10,000-square-foot facility, financed by a bond election, was named Gladys Harrington Library in honor of Harrington's meritorious service. In 2023, a $5 million renovation added a new children's area, a children's program room, a teen space, and study and meeting rooms. Pictured in 2023 are library community engagement manager Tammy Korns (right) with Libby Holtmann, director of libraries and a Plano Senior High School graduate.

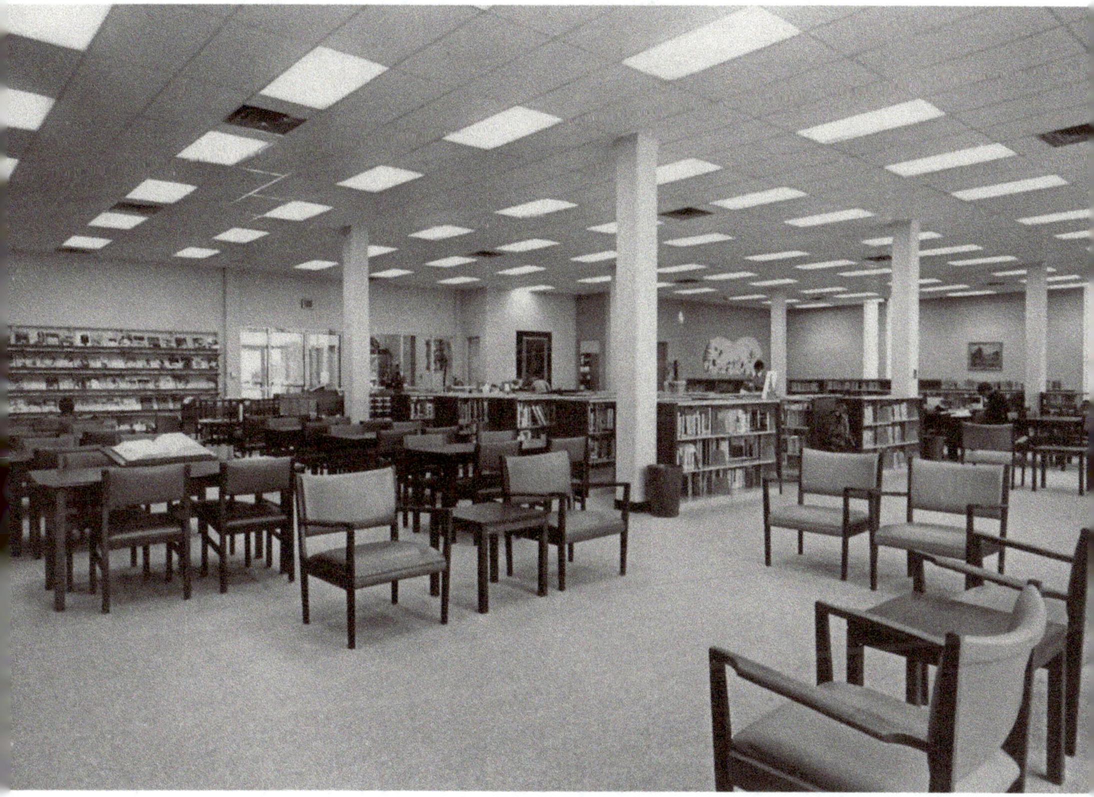

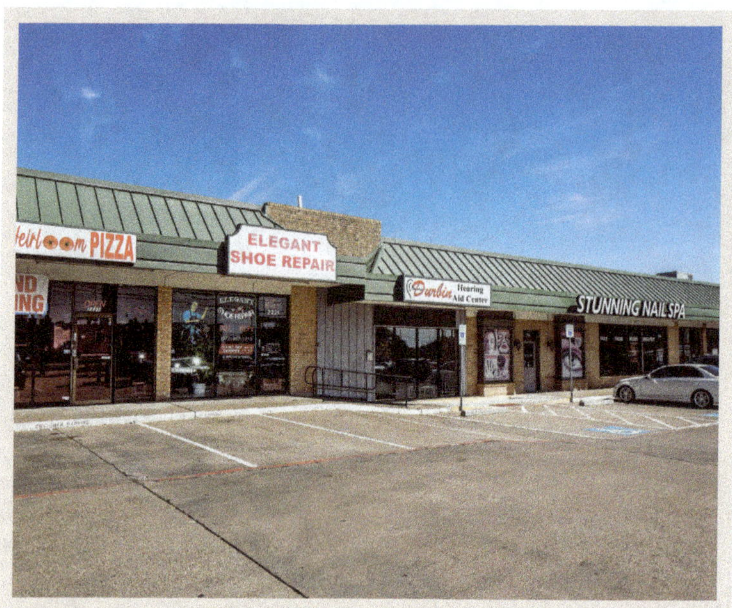


Plano's residential building boom continued in the early 1970s, and Dallas realtor Ebby Halliday saw the growth potential. A temporary office (with an outhouse) was installed on an empty lot on West 15th Street near Custer Road. Ebby realtors kept a pot of coffee ready so builders could stop by for a cup. Ebby Halliday Realtors opened a permanent office at 2213 West 15th Street in 1974; the recent photograph shows the area today. (Past, courtesy of Ebby Halliday Realtors.)

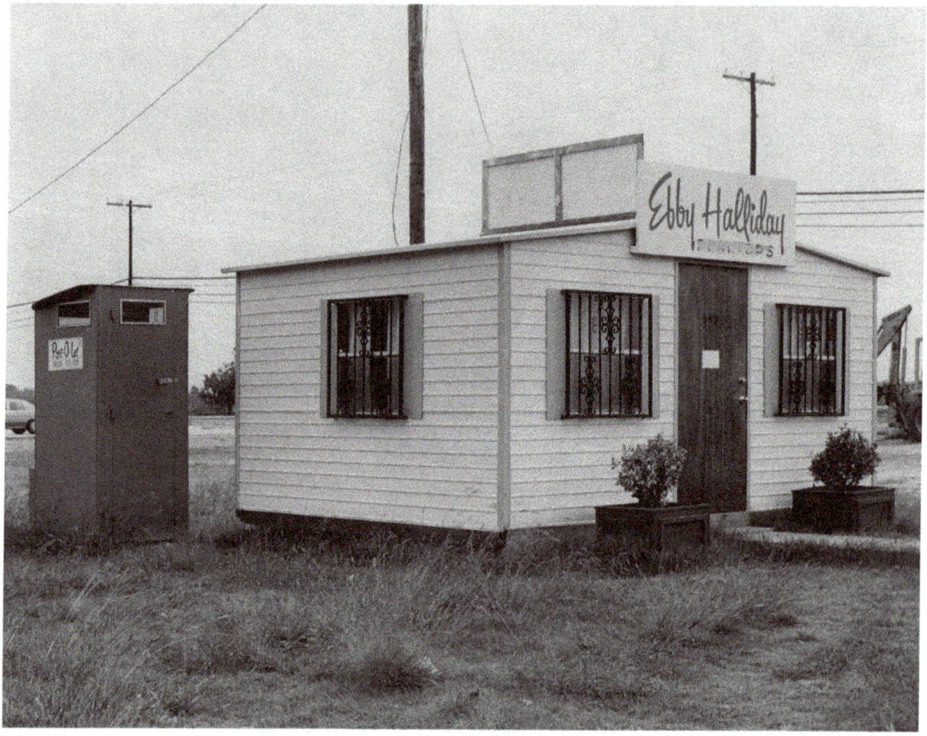

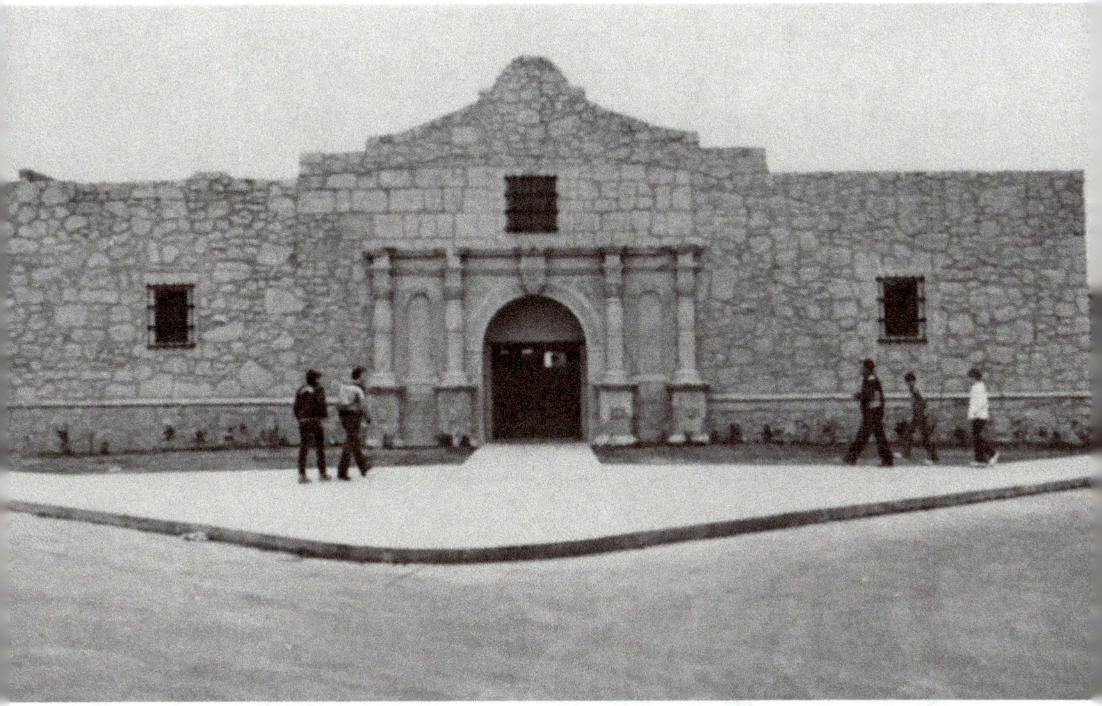

Alamo Fun Center was such a hotspot that it merited a page in Vines High School's 1983 yearbook. Teens hung out at the $1 million arcade for video games, bumper boats, miniature golf, and pizza. Today, pictured below, Crest Auto Group Collision Center occupies the building at 420 Lexington Drive. The owners say it is not uncommon to see a gaggle of international tourists snapping photographs, perhaps mistaking Plano's Alamo for the real thing. (Past, courtesy of Vines High School.)

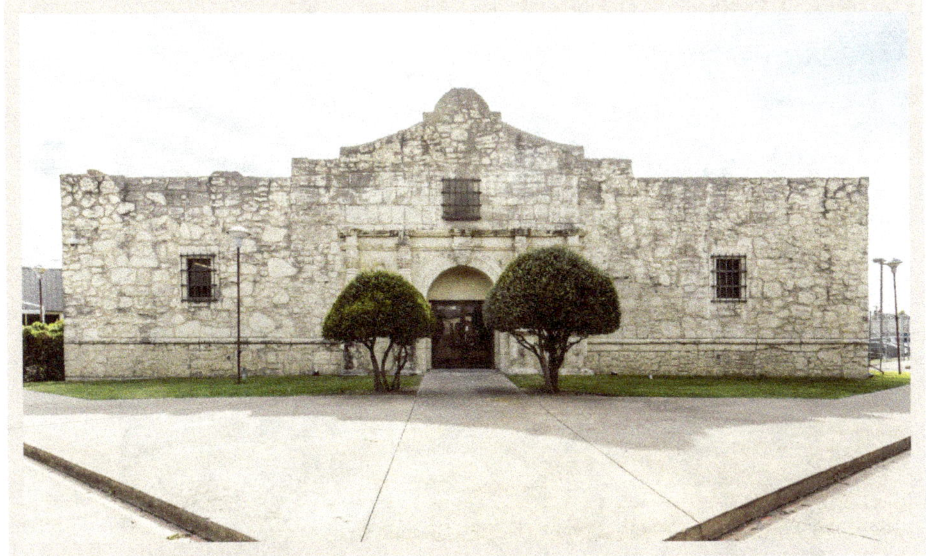

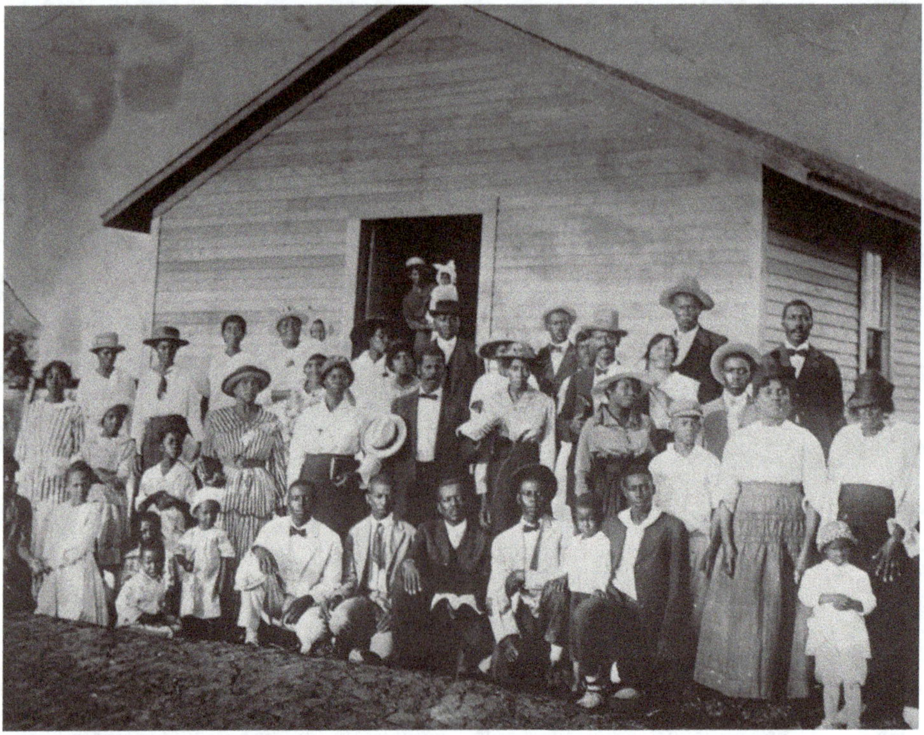

Andy Drake settled in Plano in 1864, becoming a founding father of the historically Black Douglass Community near downtown Plano. Churches were a center of social life in the community's early days and continue to be so today. Pictured are members of the Holiness Church, date unknown. Although records are unclear, residents believe the Holy Communion Outreach Temple occupies the same spot today at 1110 H Avenue. The historically Black L.A. Davis Cemetery is nearby.

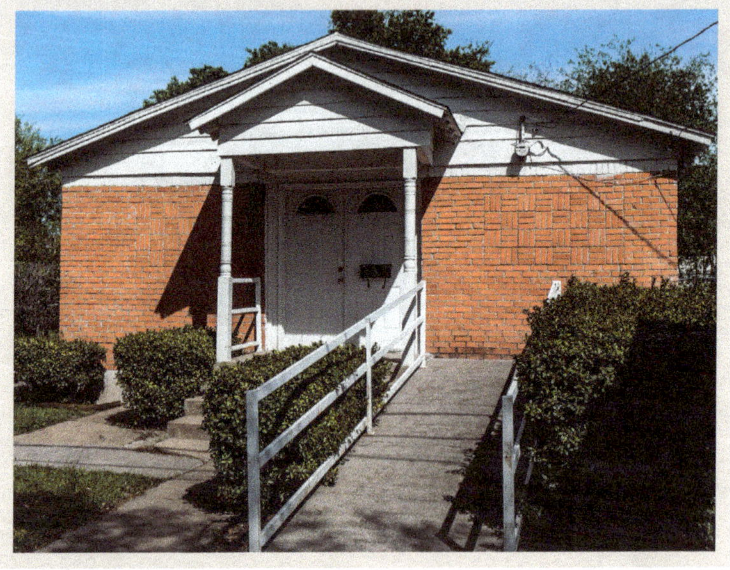

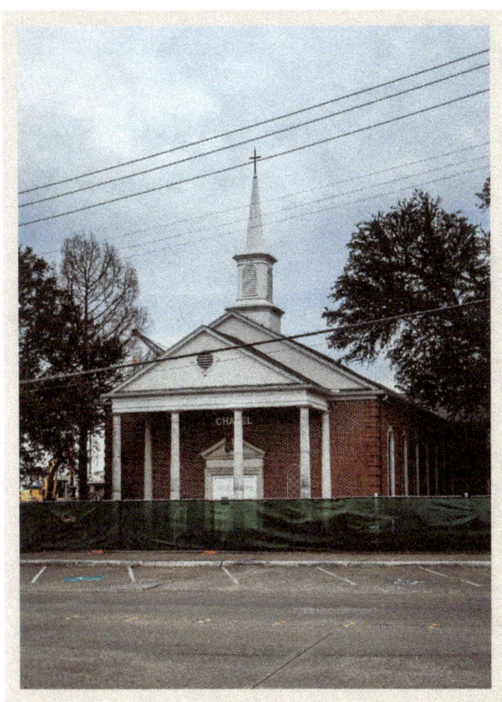

The congregation of First Baptist Church of Plano began meeting in a schoolhouse in 1852, then moved to the corner of M Avenue and 15th Street in 1897 (pictured in this early-1900s vintage image.) A new building was constructed there in 1973, and the congregation remained until 2021, when it moved to a newly constructed complex on the President George Bush Turnpike. Pictured in 2023 is the 15th Street church building after the congregation moved out.

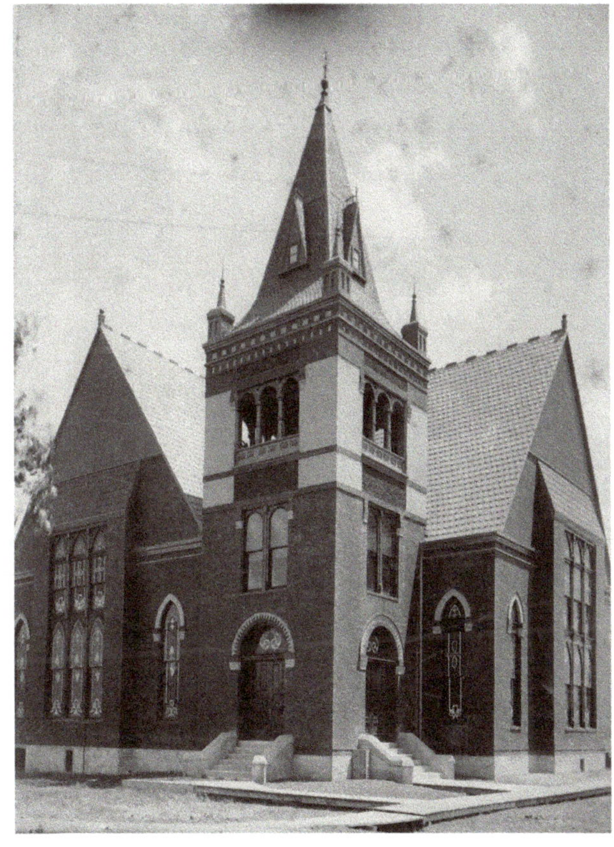

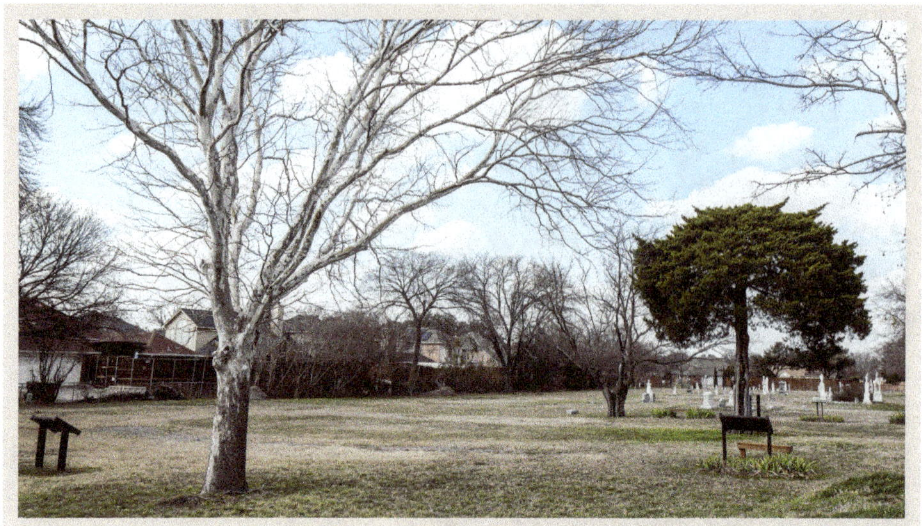

Bethany Christian Church, founded in 1876 by Capt. R.W. Carpenter and Capt. W.N. Bush, was a center of community life, with box suppers, community singings, and theatrical productions. Many early residents fondly remembered the decorated 16-foot Christmas tree that graced the sanctuary every December. Attendance dwindled in the 1930s as road improvements gave easier access to town. Today, all that remains is Bethany Cemetery near Custer Road and Cannes Drive.

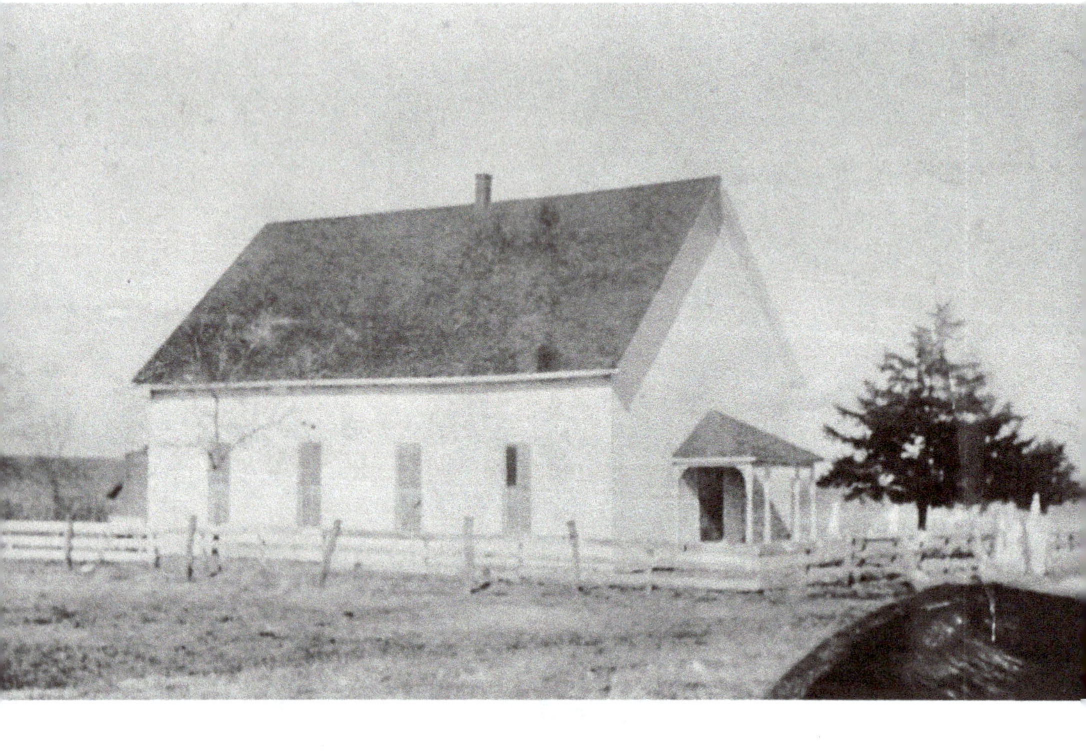

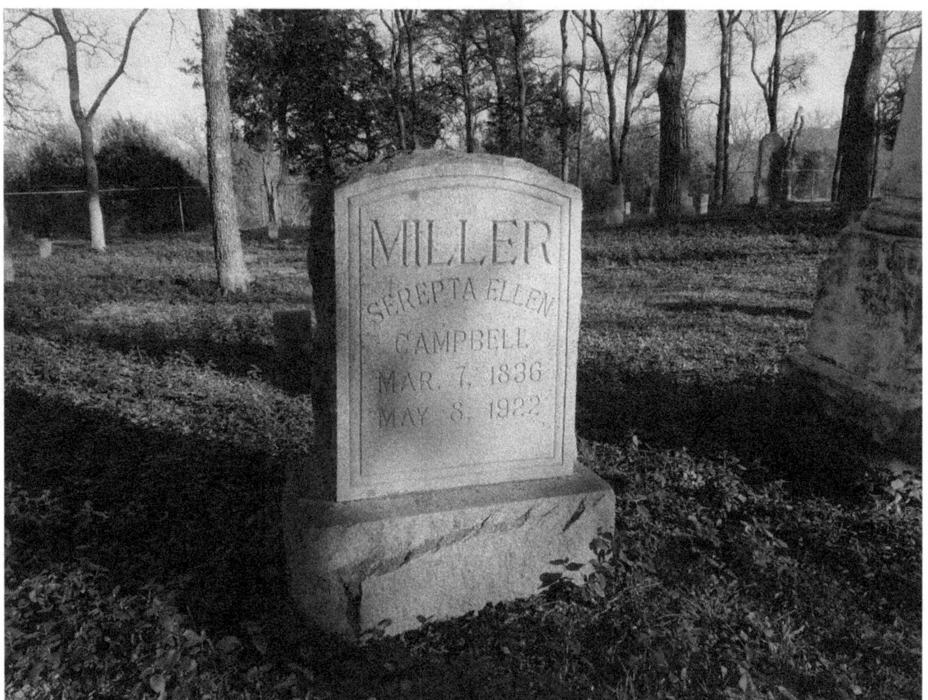


Routh Cemetery is one of the oldest burial grounds in Collin County. Jacob Routh, a Baptist preacher, bought the land in 1852; his mother, Elizabeth, and only son, John, are buried here. It is technically located in Richardson (south of Renner Road and east of Central Expressway), but many pioneers from Plano and surrounding communities were buried here. In recent years, new apartments and walking trails have surrounded the once-remote cemetery. (Past, photograph by Jeff Campbell.)

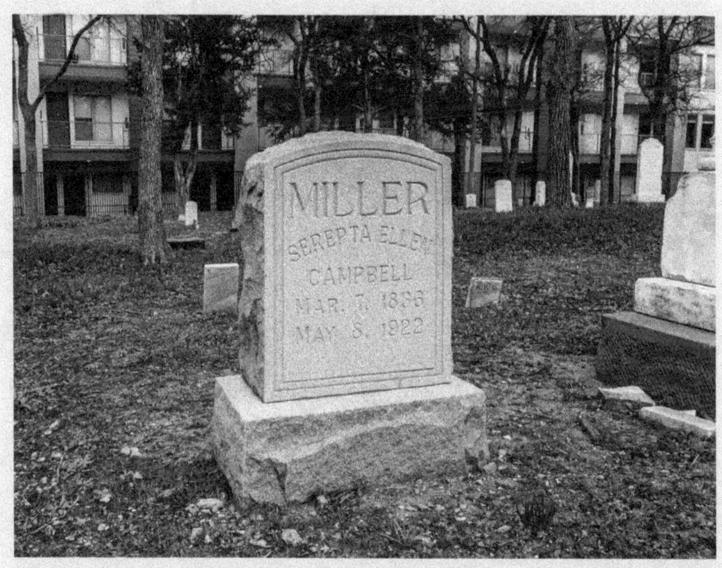

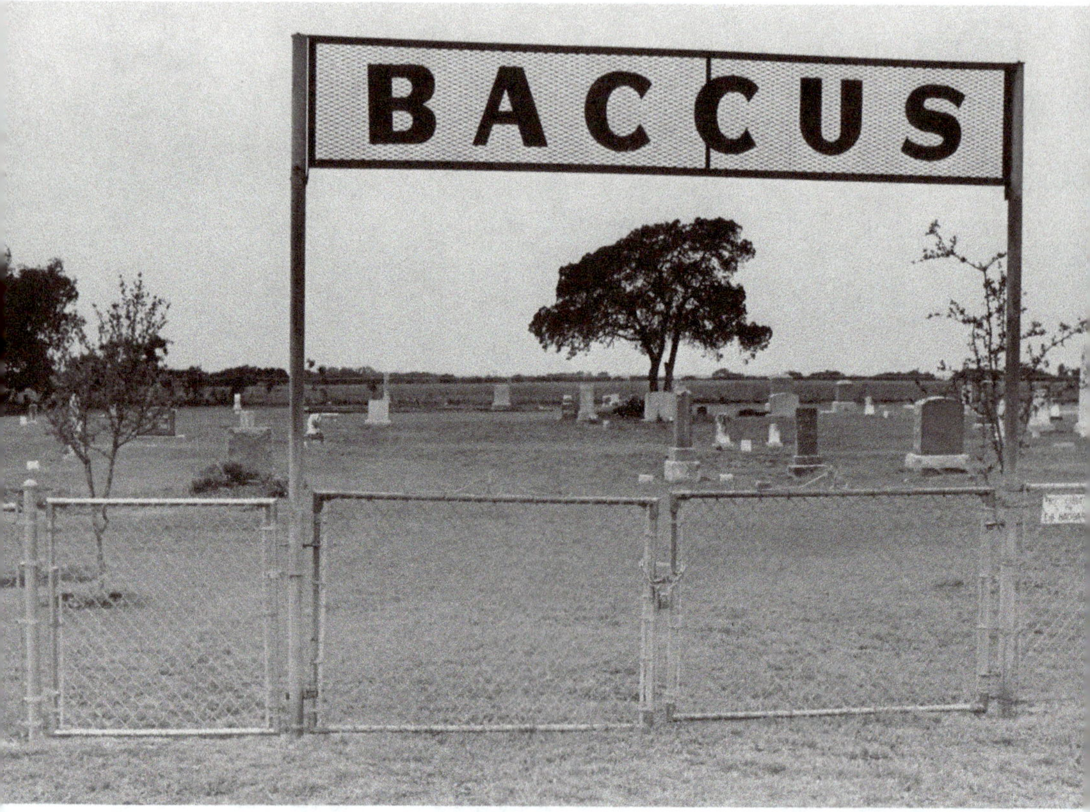

Located near the Shawnee Trail (now Preston Road), the Baccus Cemetery originally served as a family plot for war veteran Henry Cook in 1845. Cook came to Texas with some of the earliest pioneers of Plano—the Peters Colonists. By 1915, the cemetery was renamed Baccus Cemetery, after Cook's daughter, Rachel Baccus, who donated the land. When the Shops at Legacy were built, Baccus Cemetery was preserved and remains today in the center of the shopping area.

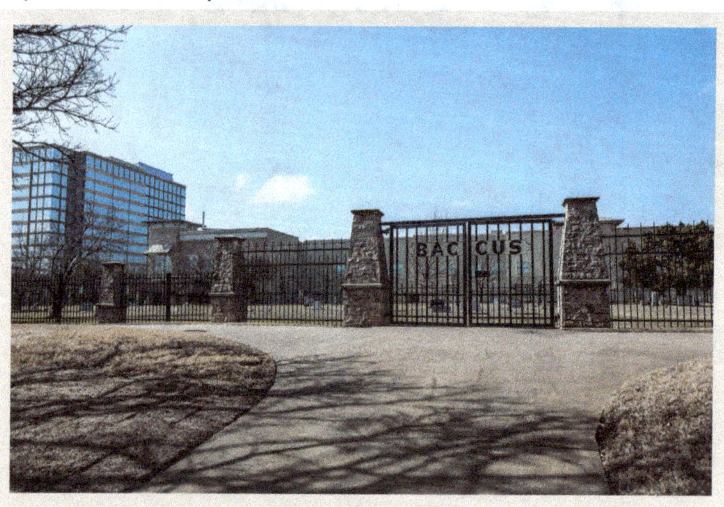

CHAPTER 5

# HOMES

## *FOUNDING FAMILIES*

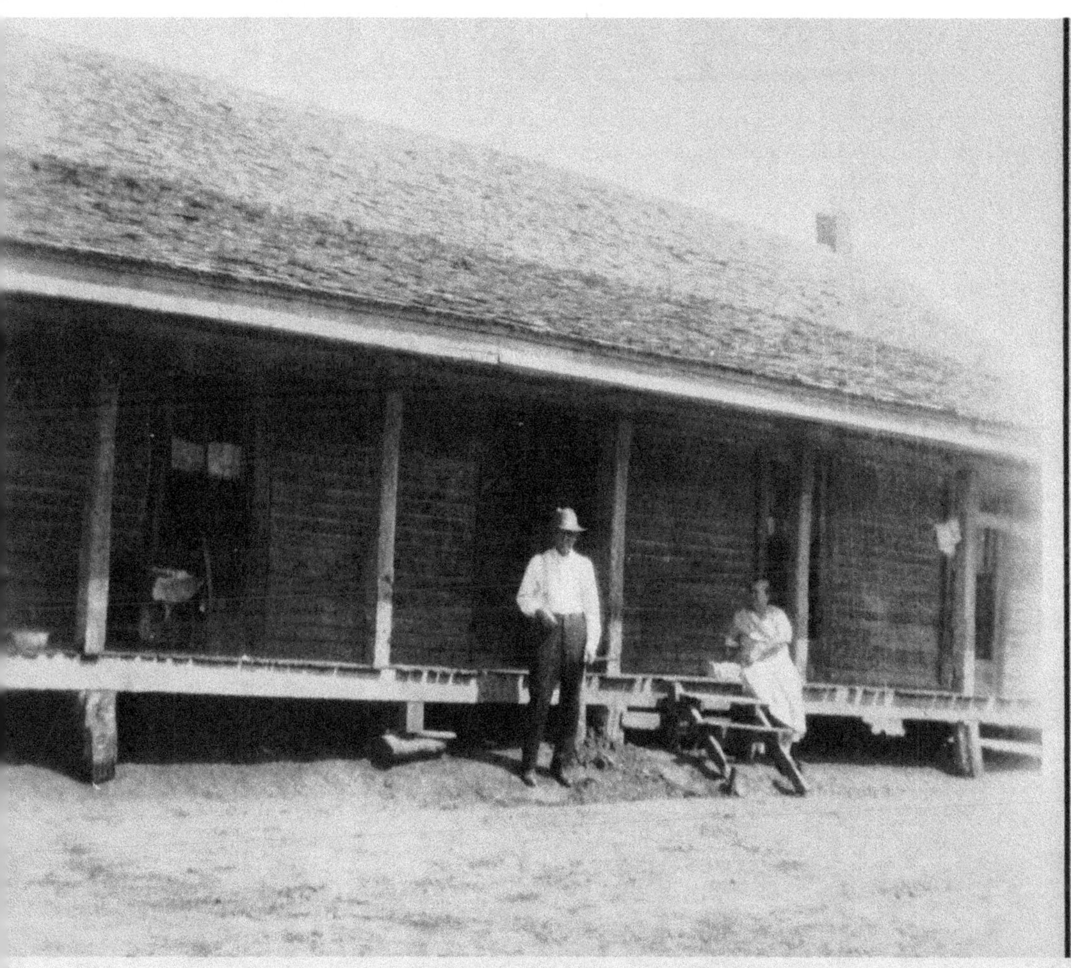

Plano residents have always taken pride in their houses. This early home did double duty: a residence for William Forman I's family and a post office. Shortly after arriving from Kentucky, Forman became Plano's first official postmaster in 1852. Today, a shopping center occupies the corner of 14th Street and Jupiter Road, near where the Forman house once stood.

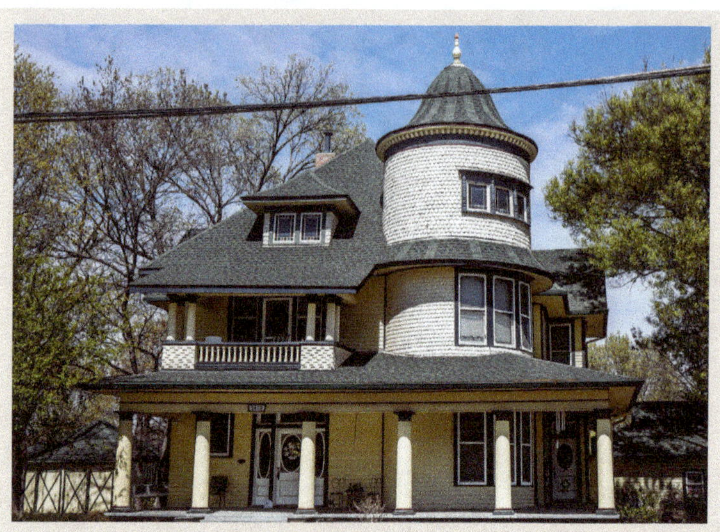

This home at 1413 East 15th Street was built in 1901 by A.G. McAdams, an architect and lumber dealer who moved with his family to Plano from St. Louis, Missouri. Later, the home was purchased by E.J. Roller and has been known as the Roller House ever since. Roller was one of the founding stockholders of First Guaranty State Bank of Plano, chartered in 1910 and taken over by Plano National Bank in 1917.

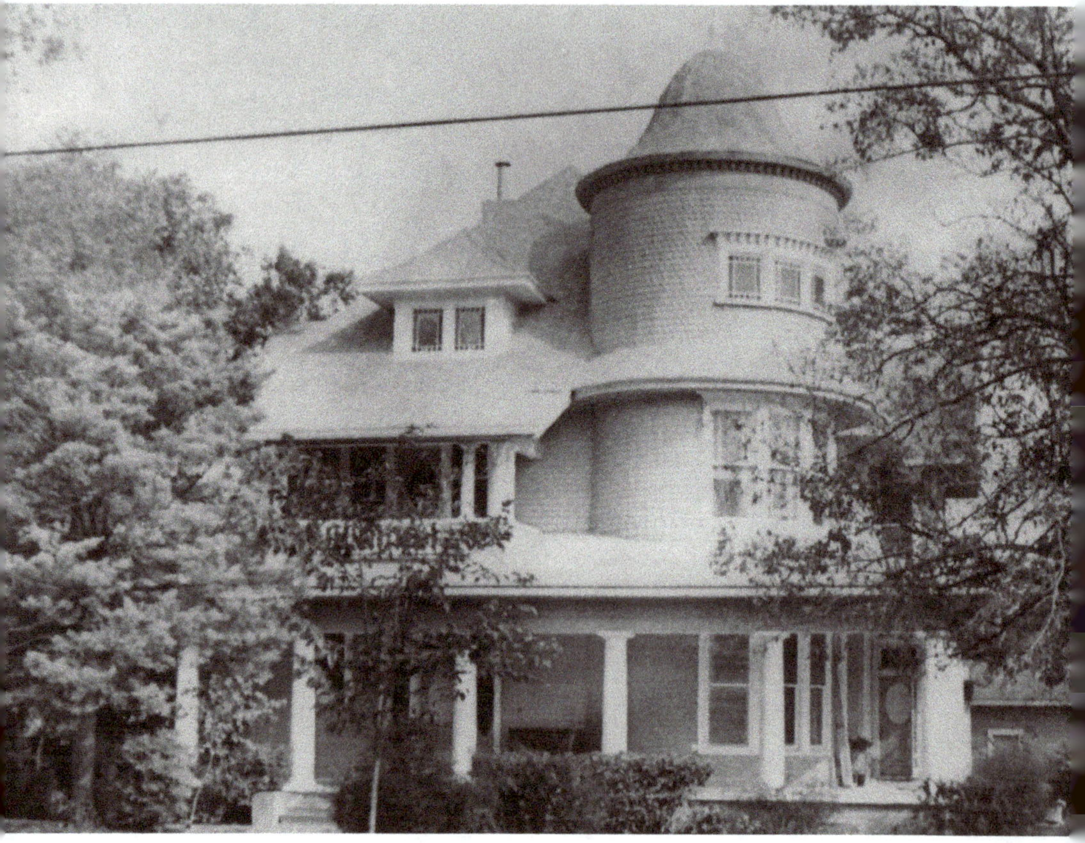

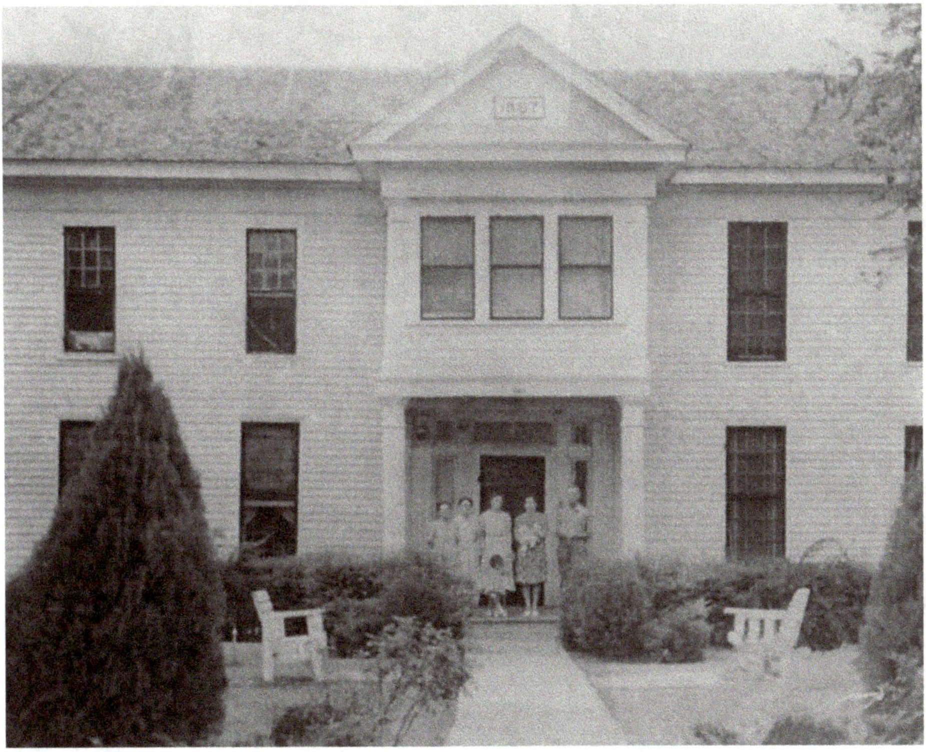

Joe and Elizabeth Forman built this home in 1867; today, it is one of the oldest homes still standing in Plano, located at 1617 K Avenue. Over the years, the Greek Revival structure has served as a residence, a stagecoach stop, and an apartment house. Pictured in 2023 is Gwen Workman, owner of the Wooden Spoon, a shop selling Scandinavian items and an informal Scandinavian cultural center. The vintage photograph is from the 1930s. (Past, courtesy of Gwen Workman.)

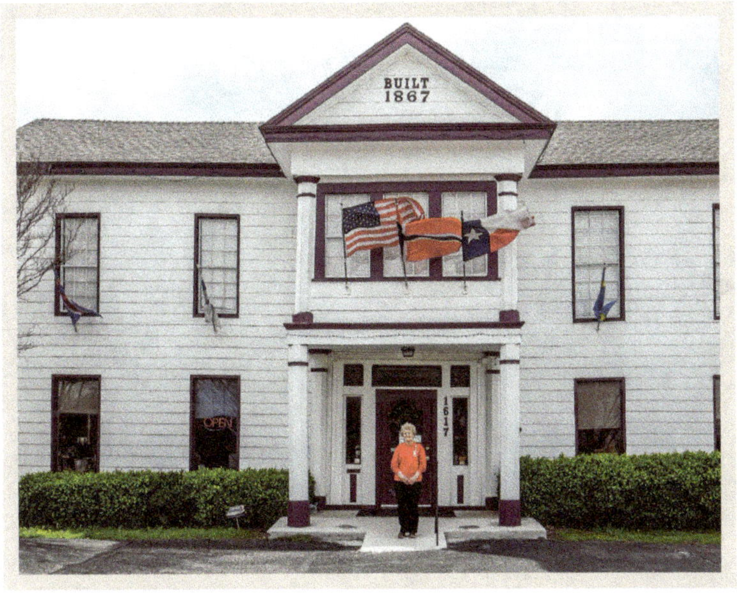

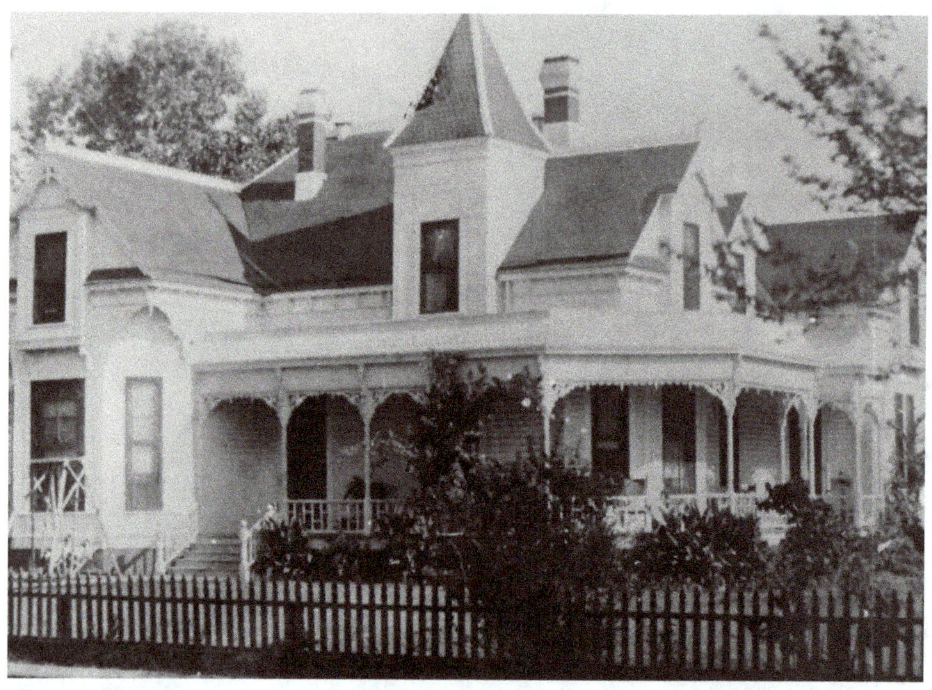

The home of Silas M. Harrington once stood at the corner of West 15th Street and Columbia Place. Silas, born in 1862, was a civic leader, a family man, and an active member of the Methodist Church, where he taught the Baraca men's class. He also owned Harrington Pharmacy in downtown Plano. Today, office buildings occupy the spot where the home once stood.

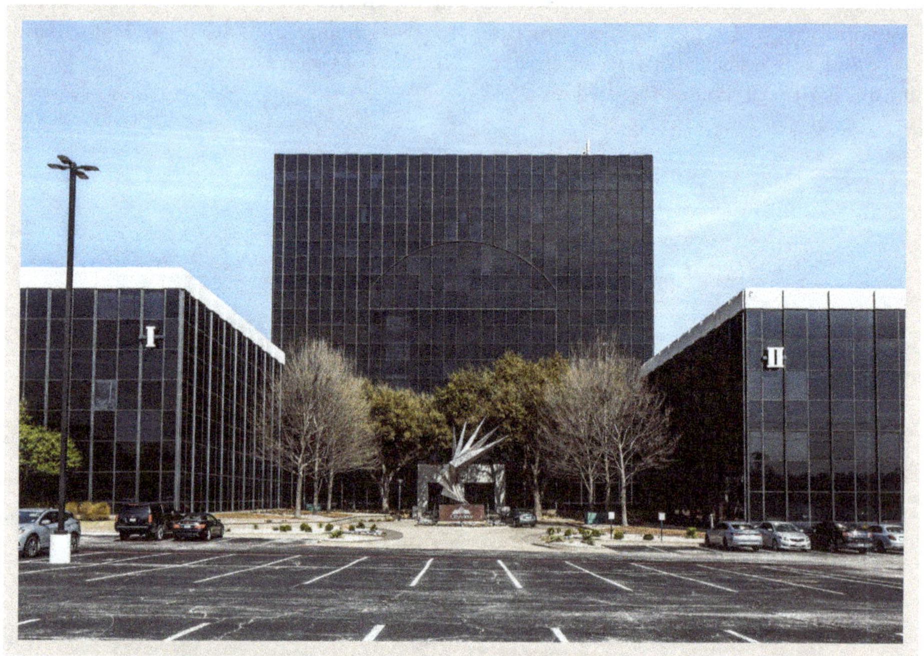

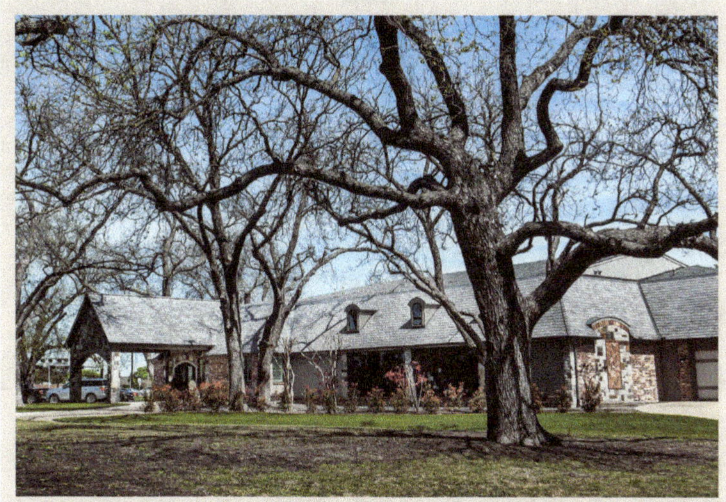

The John Harrington house was located near the southwest corner of what is now Custer Road and Spring Creek Parkway. The vintage photograph was likely taken in the early 1920s. Harrington married Mary Frances "Fannie" Mathews, a dedicated churchwoman for whom the Fannie Harrington Methodist Chapel was named. The chapel was torn down in 1962 when the church was dissolved. Today, Allen Family Funeral Options and Custer Road Church of Christ occupy the area where the John Harrington House once stood.

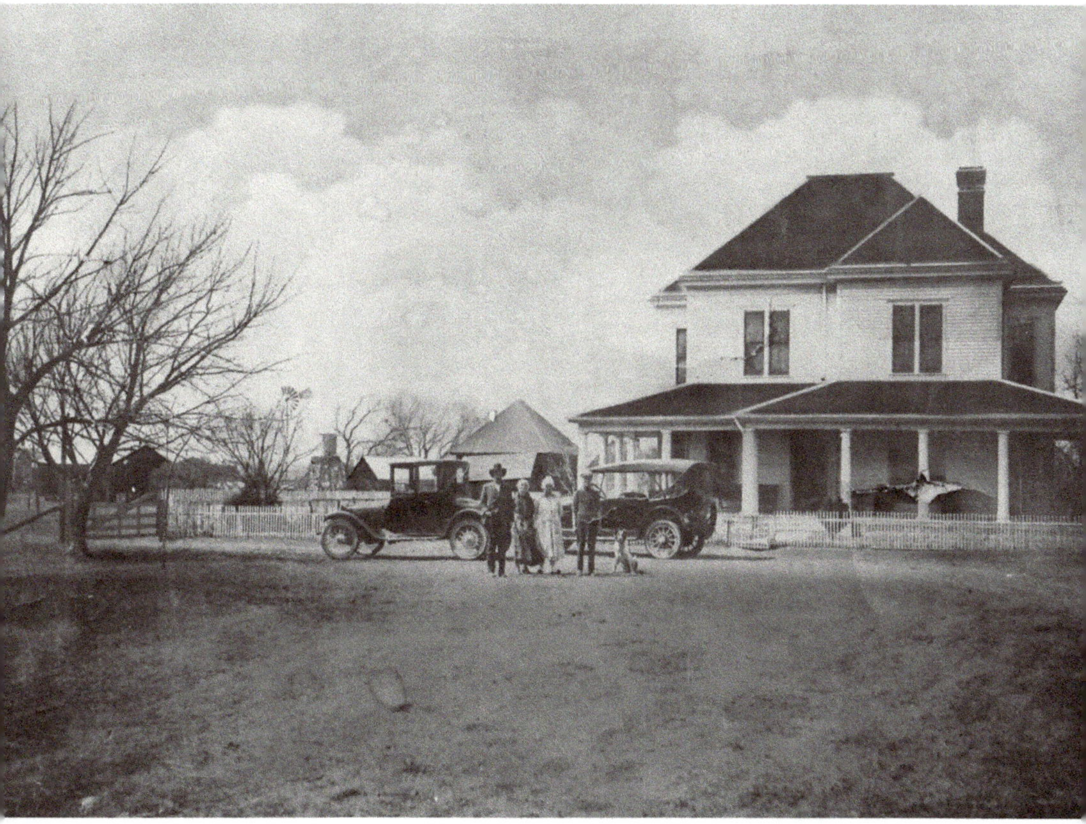

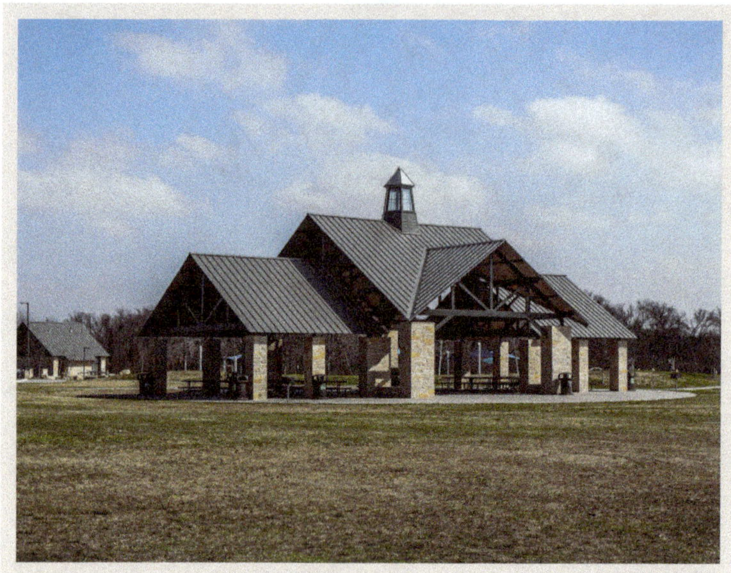

The Haggard-Fox House (previously known as the Collinwood House) was the home of Clinton Shepard "C.S." Haggard and Nancy Catherine Lunsford "Nannie Kate" Haggard, purchased from the Fox brothers in 1862. Preservationists discovered this was the oldest existing house in Plano—possibly pre–Civil War—in 2014, just as the city prepared to demolish it. In 2018, the house was relocated to Haggard farmland. Pictured in 2023 is Windhaven Meadows Park, built on the land where the Haggard-Fox House previously stood.

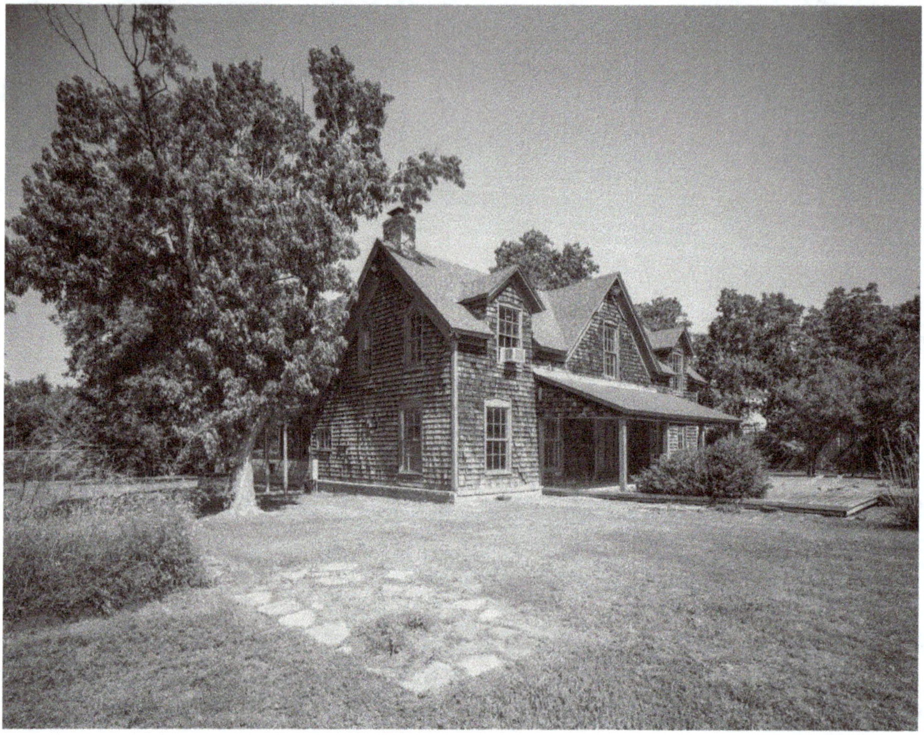

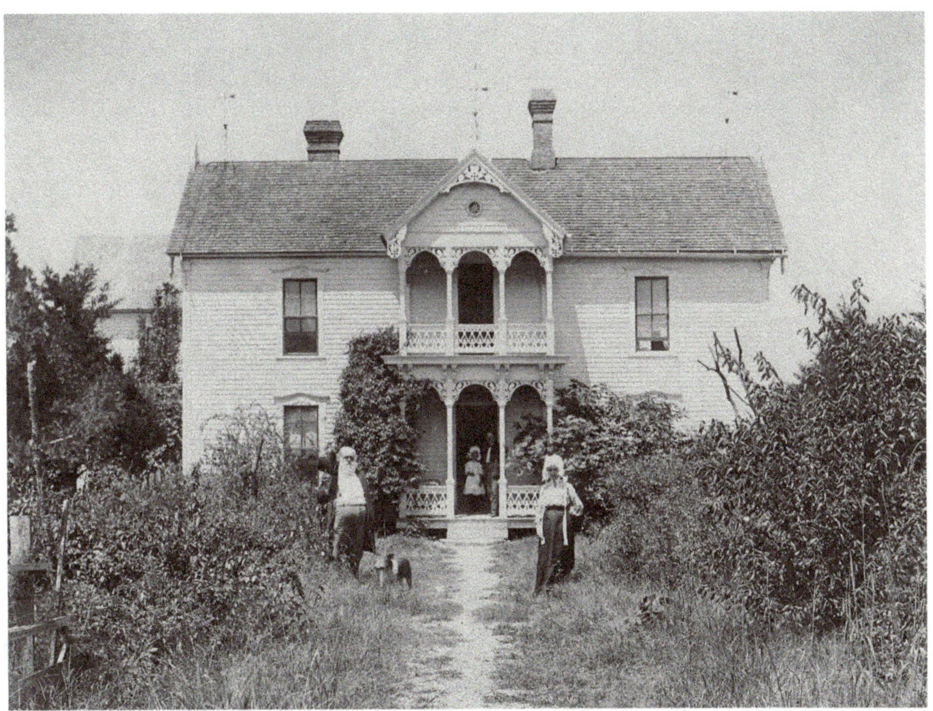

Members of the Haggard family have lived at this farm near Park Boulevard and Custer Road since 1884, when C.S. and Nannie Kate built their new house. That original home was remodeled in the 1930s by W.O. Haggard Sr. and his wife, Rosa, and then torn down in 1967, with a new home built for W.O. Haggard Jr. and his wife, Merle. Haggard family members still live there today. Residential development has filled the northern pasture where cattle once grazed.

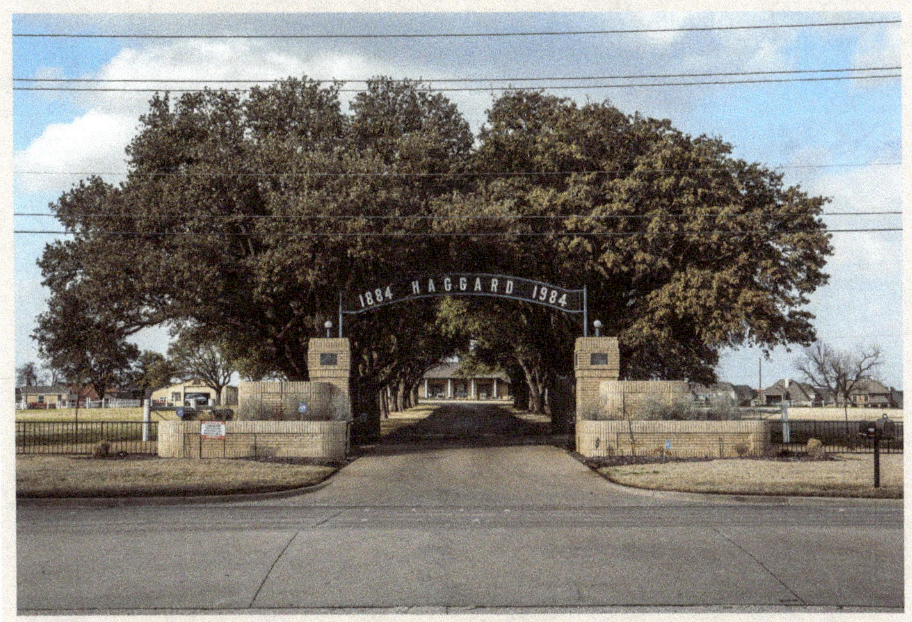

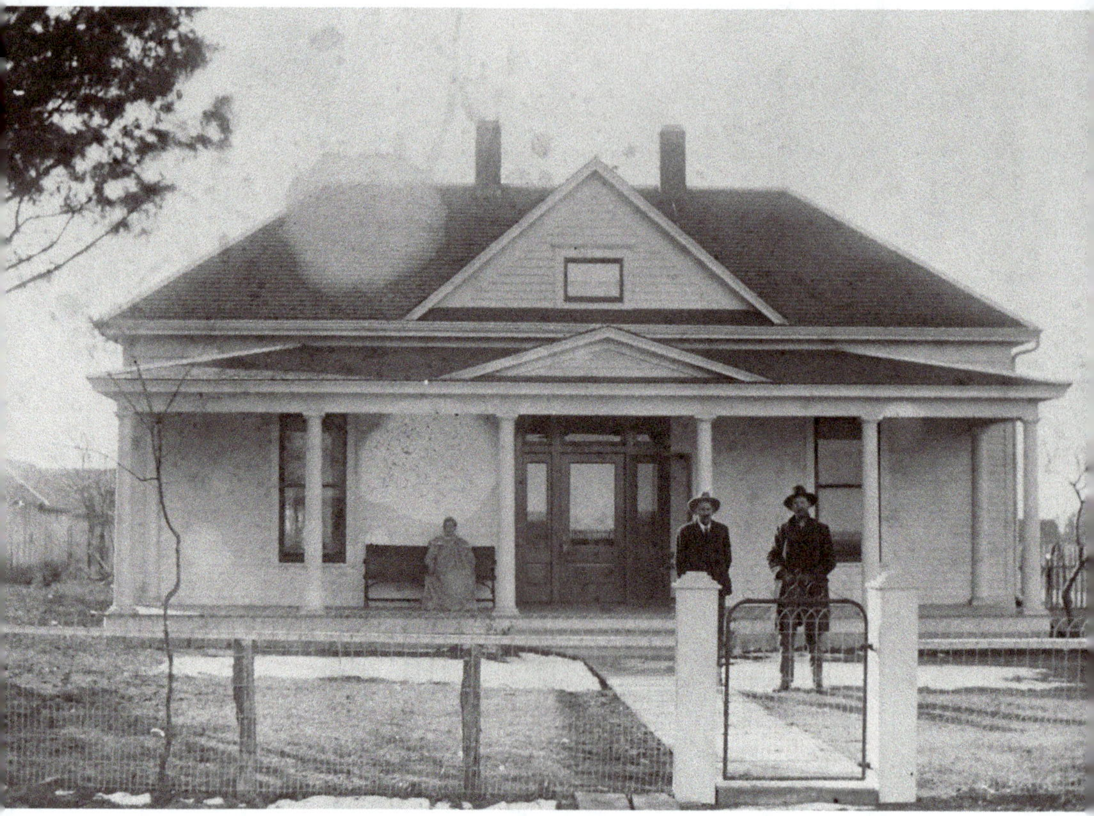

Pictured in the vintage image is the William Joel "W.J." Carpenter home at 708 East 16th Street, with (from left to right) Emma B. Carpenter, W.J., and B.B. Carpenter Sr. in 1908. William's father, Robert Washington Carpenter, was among Plano's earliest settlers and a large donor in support of Add-Ran College, now Texas Christian University. The house was later widened to add a bathroom and kitchen in the 1940s and 1950s. The house is currently owned by descendants of the Carpenter family.

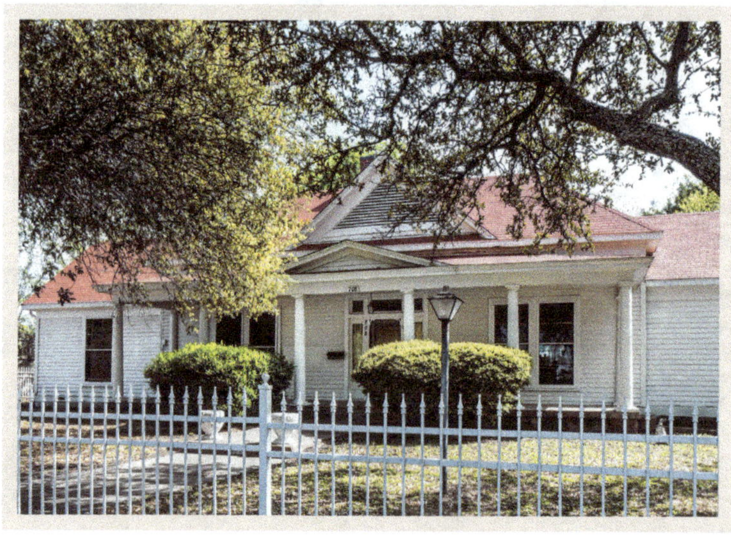

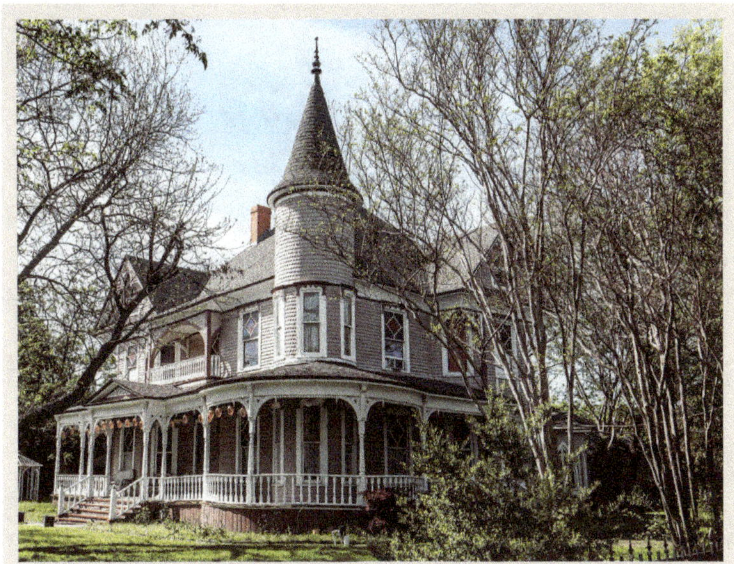

This Queen Anne Victorian mansion (on 16th Street at M Avenue) was built in 1898 for Col. Henry C. Overaker and his new bride. After Overaker died, the property was bought in 1919 by Gibson Carpenter, a prominent teacher, lawyer, and farmer, and remained in the Carpenter family until the 1950s. In the 1990s and 2000s, the Carpenter House was an event venue for weddings. The home is privately owned today. (Past, courtesy of Joan Keagy.)

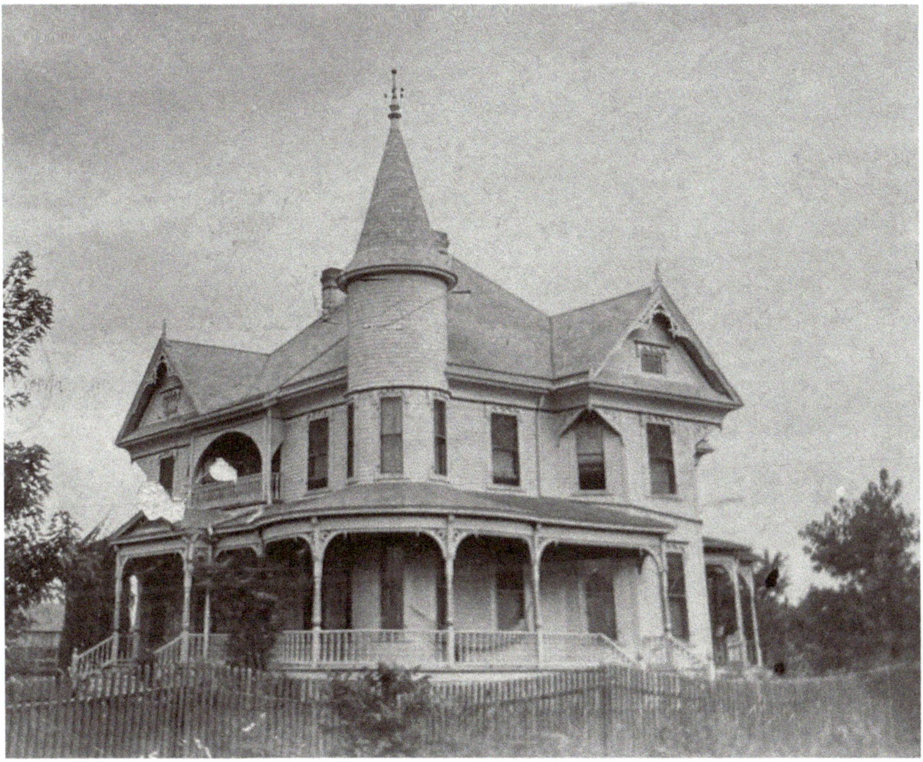

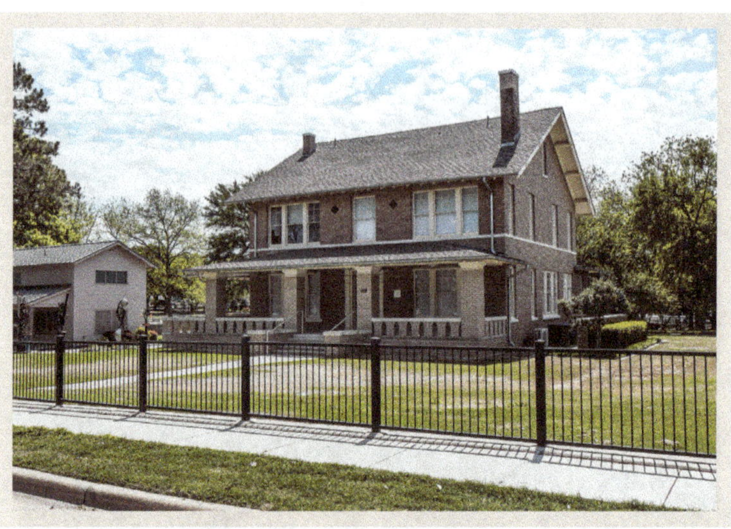

This home was built in 1917 for Celestine Saigling, the widow of C.F. Saigling, a prominent citizen who owned lumberyards, sawmills, and flour mills in Plano. Celestine remained there until her death in 1932; Dr. O.T. Mitchell owned the home when the c. 1940 vintage image was taken. In 2017, the Saigling House at 902 East 16th Street was renovated and became the ArtCentre of Plano, a gallery and events venue. (Past, courtesy of the ArtCentre of Plano.)

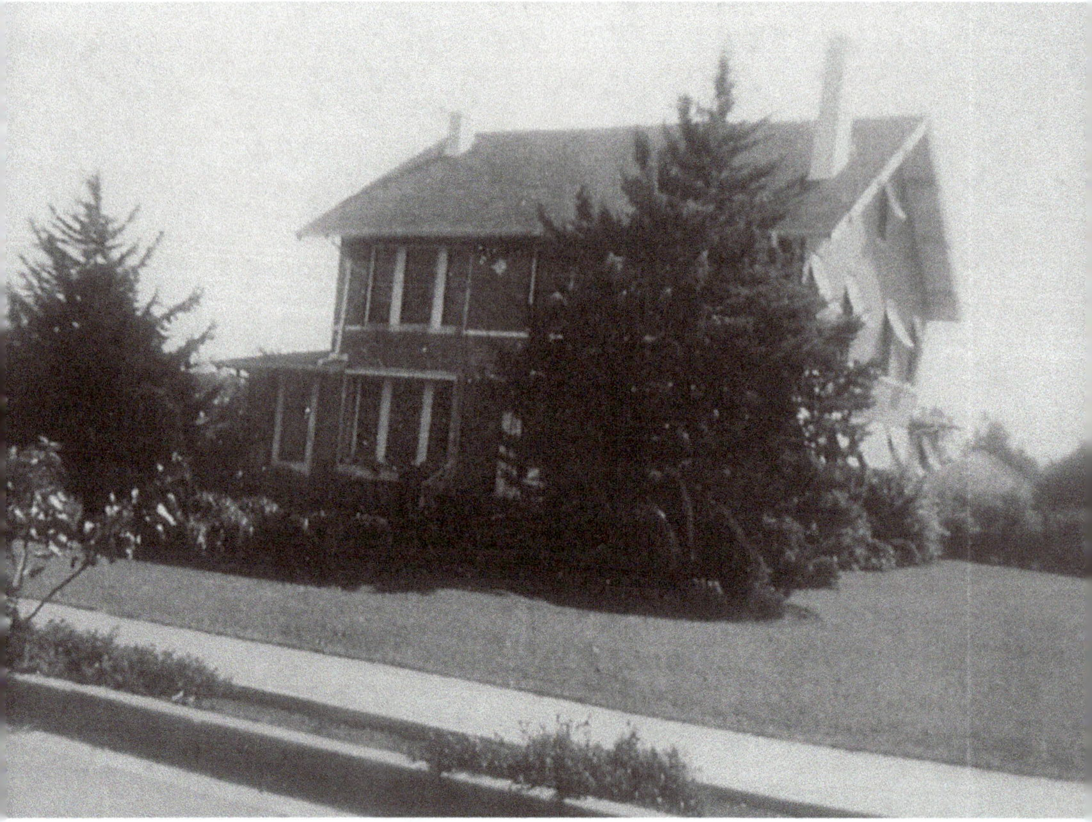

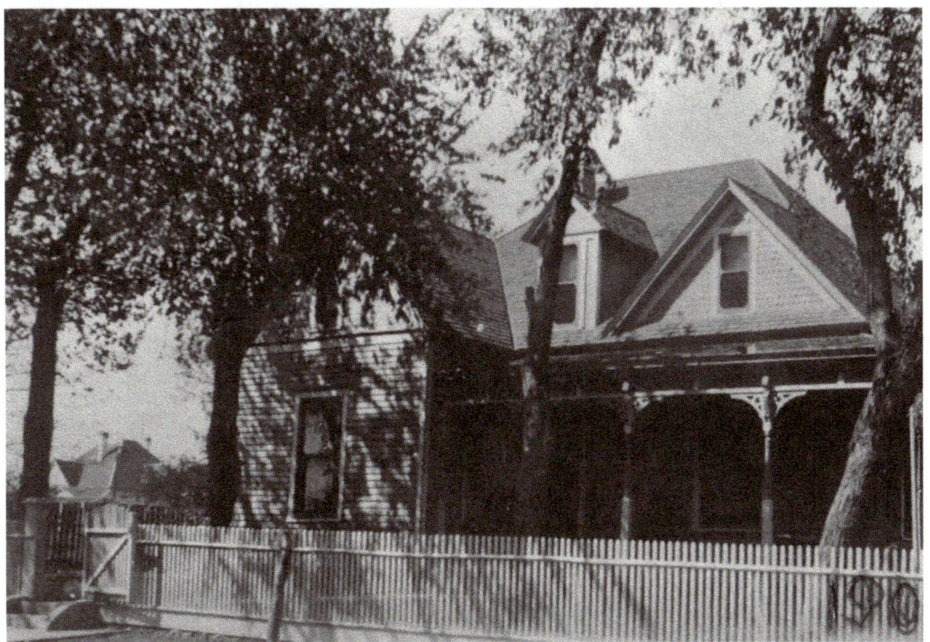


Elizabeth "Lizzie" Smoot (1834–1914) lived in this house at 909 East 16th Street with her son John and niece Mattie Hulse. John was a doctor at Baylor Hospital and later taught at Baylor Medical School. The house still stands and is a private residence. Granny Smoot, as she was affectionately known to many, was active in keeping Plano's cemeteries in good condition. She is buried in Plano Mutual Cemetery.

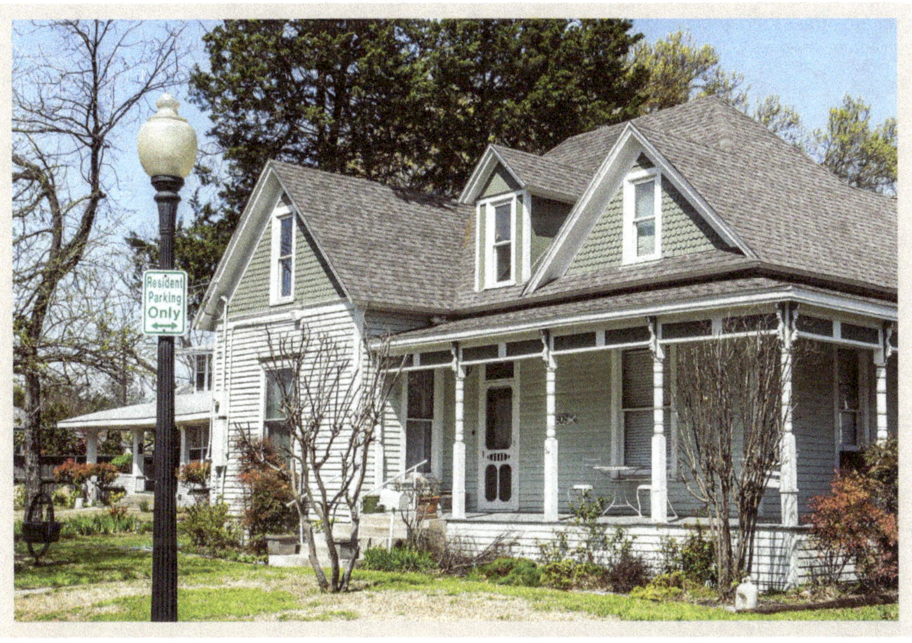

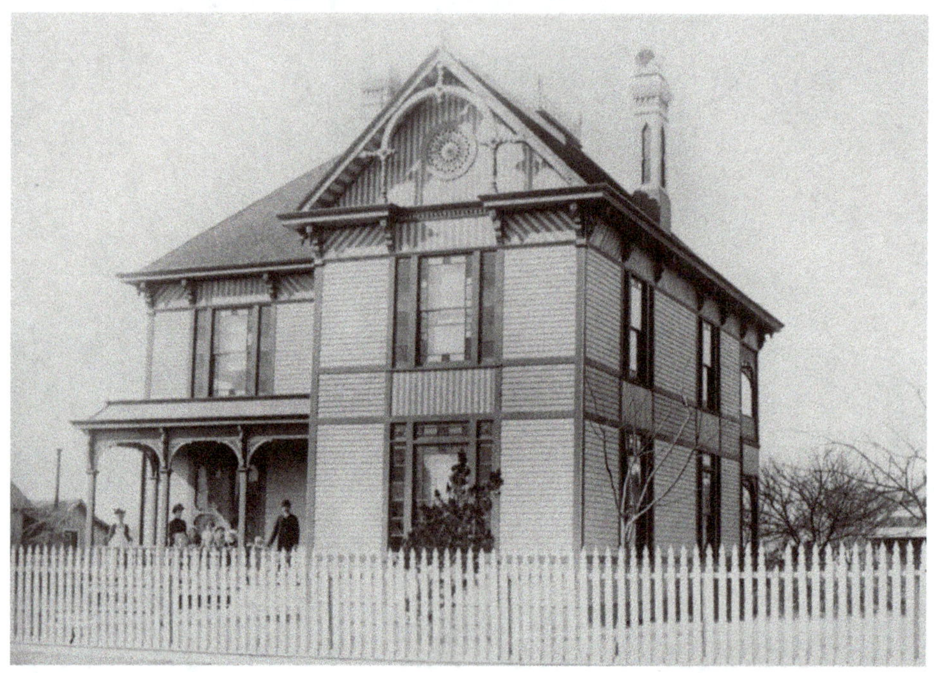

Frederick Schimelpfenig and his wife, Louise, came from Kentucky to Plano in 1878 and, soon after, opened F. Schimelpfenig Dry Goods downtown. Fire destroyed the businesses in 1881 and again in 1895. Perhaps that inspired Fred to spearhead the laying of water mains and the distribution of water to homes and businesses during his stint as mayor (1902–1908). Today, the area where the home stood is occupied by Morada Plano Apartments near K Avenue and 14th Street.

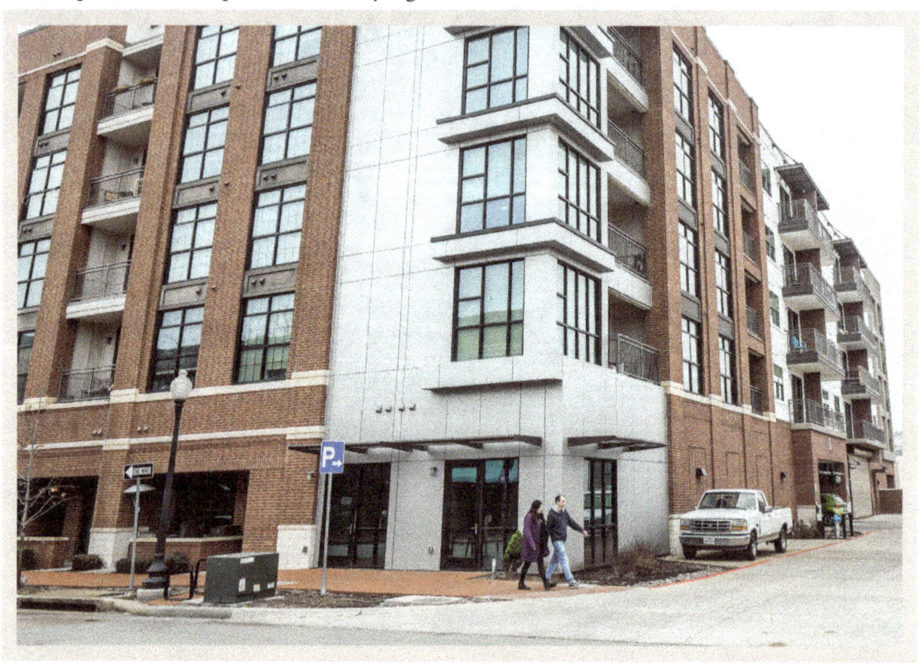

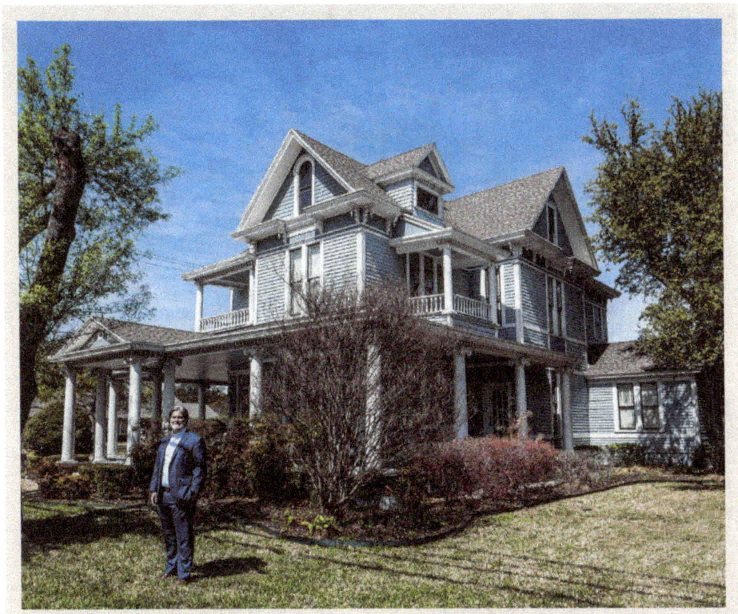

This two-story Victorian-style home at 901 East 18th Street was built in 1890 for the family of Olney Davis, a prominent businessman, civic leader, and mayor of Plano. In 1899, Davis became the first president of the board of trustees for the Plano School System. The building was converted to office use in the mid-1980s. Pictured in 2023 is David Stolle, PISD board president (2021–2023) and an Olney Davis Elementary alumnus.

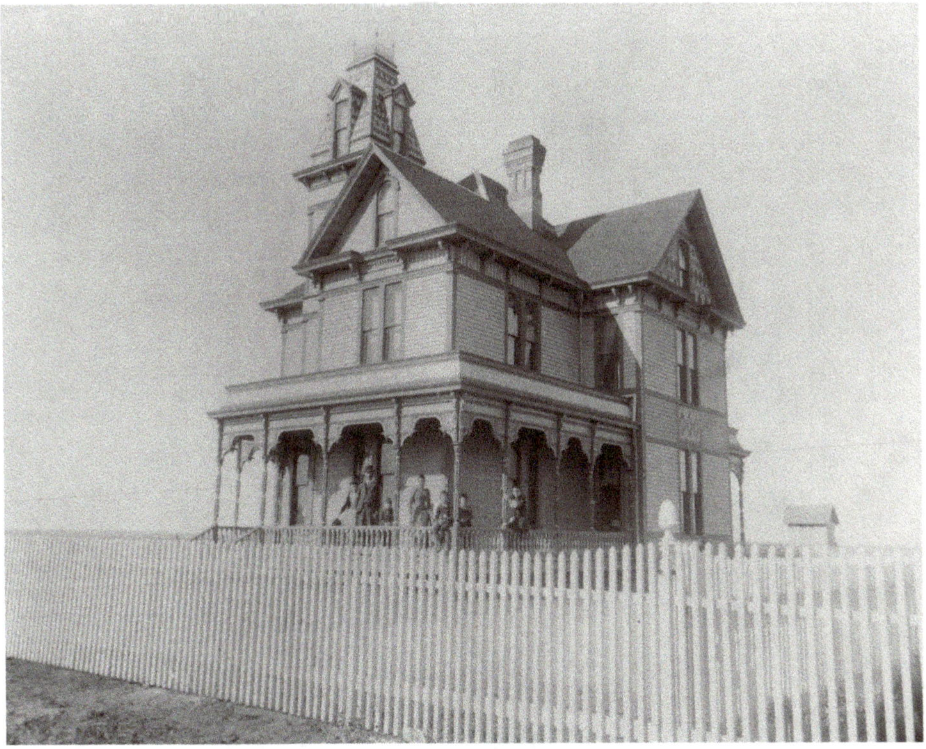

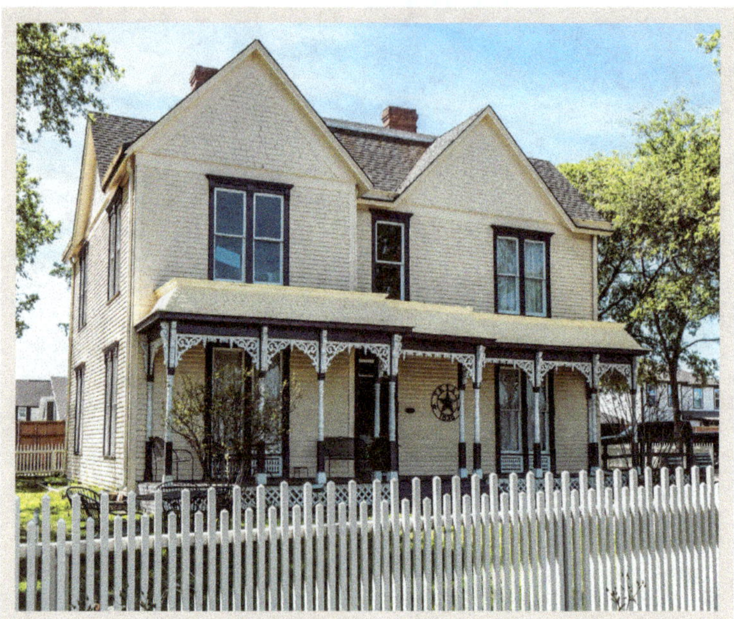

William Henry Lafayette Wells built the Wells Homestead at 3921 Coit Road in 1893. Wells came to Plano from Virginia after serving in the Civil War. For his first job, he helped drive mules, saving up enough money to purchase the homestead in 1874. Sip & Savor restaurant was here for almost 10 years but closed in 2020, citing the pandemic. Homestead Winery, the oldest operating winery in the Red River Valley of North Texas, opened a tasting room here in 2021.

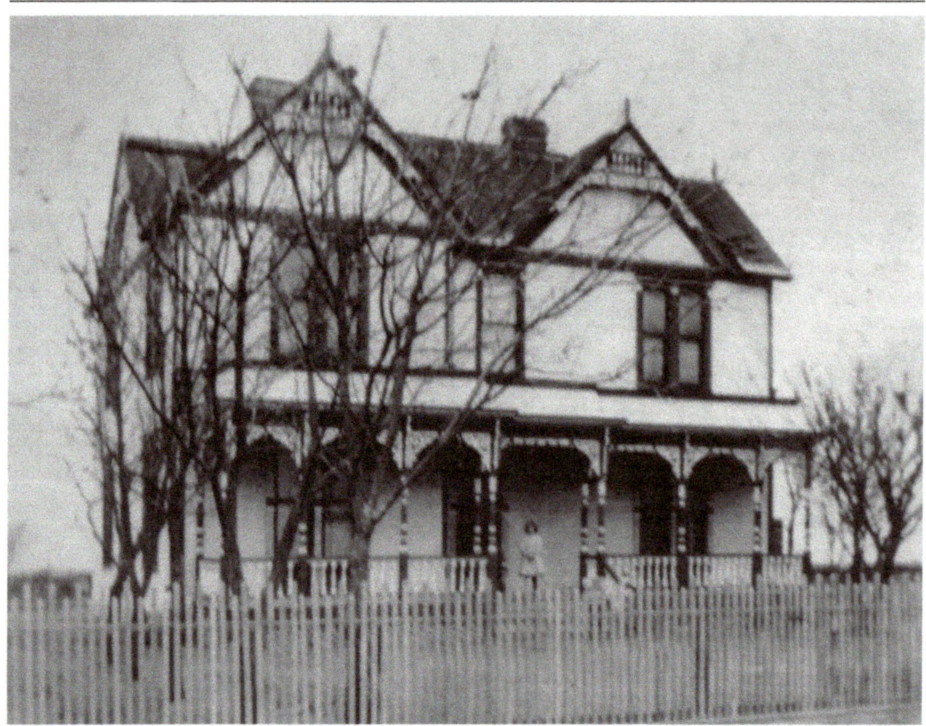

CHAPTER 6

# Schools and Sports
## Reading, Writing, and Winning

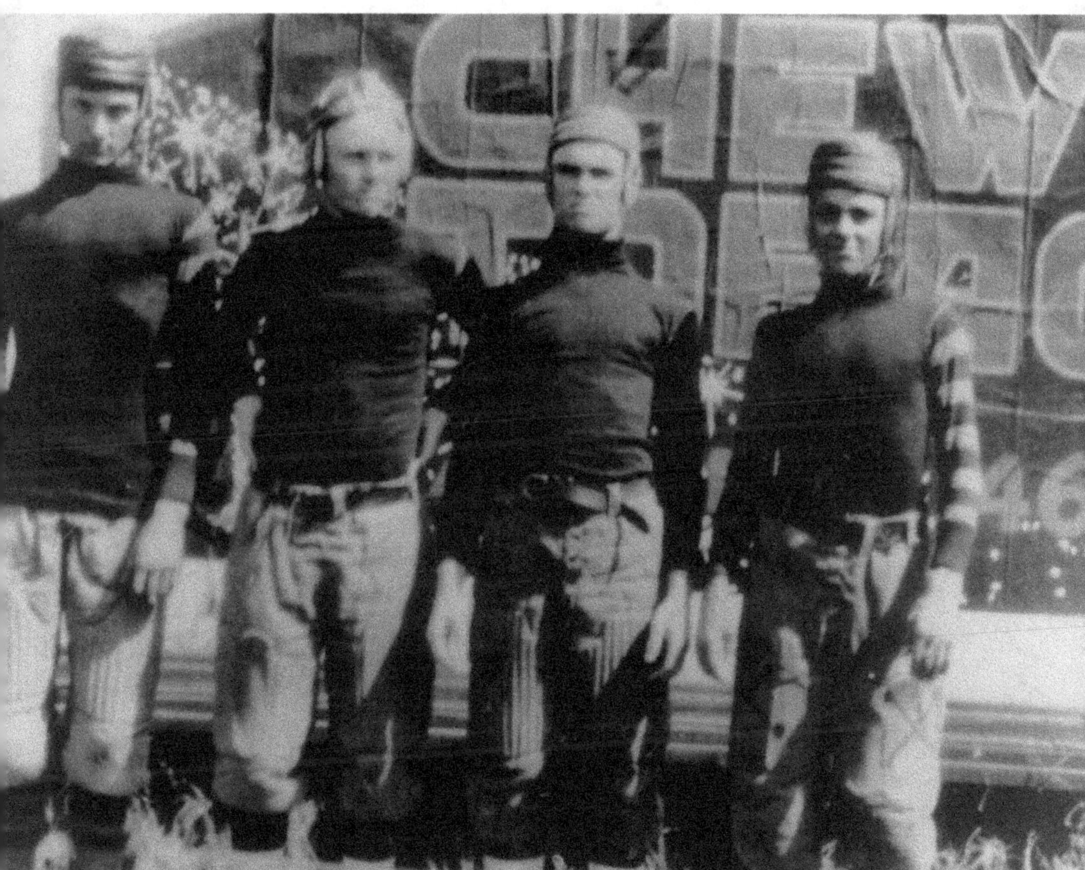

Pictured are backfield players on Plano's high school football team around 1916; from left to right are John Stults, Nelson Brigham, Madison Norton, and James Hayes.

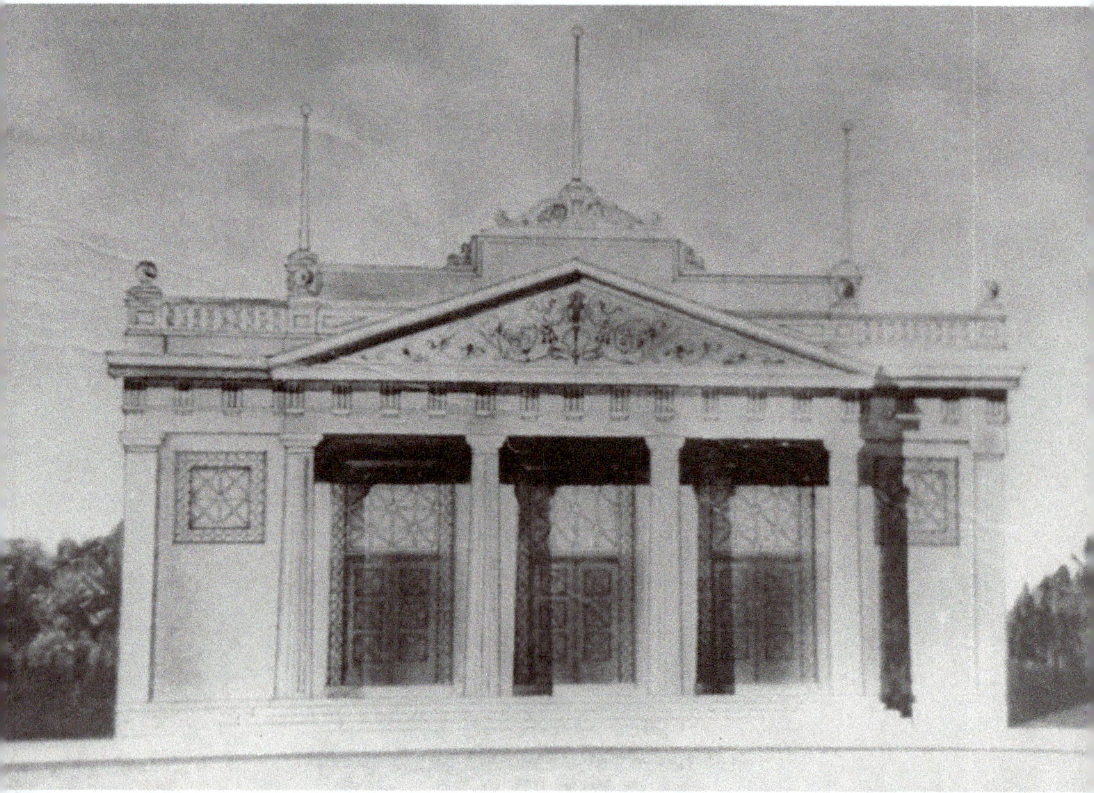

Built in 1909, the Civic Auditorium was home to a Lyceum in winter and a Chautauqua in summer—both popular early-20th-century adult educational confabs. After the auditorium was demolished, a new high school was built nearby in 1924, and in 1938, a new gym-auditorium was added. Today, that addition is home to the city of Plano's Courtyard Theater. Pictured in 2023 are Plano Arts and Events staff members with downtown Plano manager Michelle Hawkins (sixth from left.)

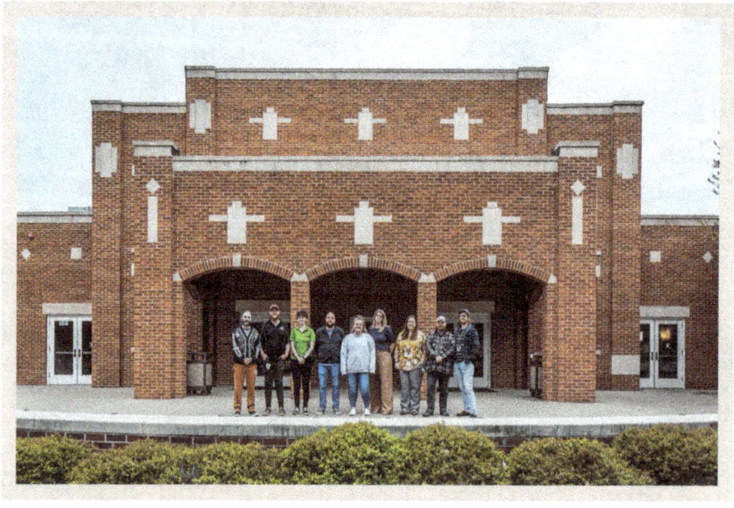

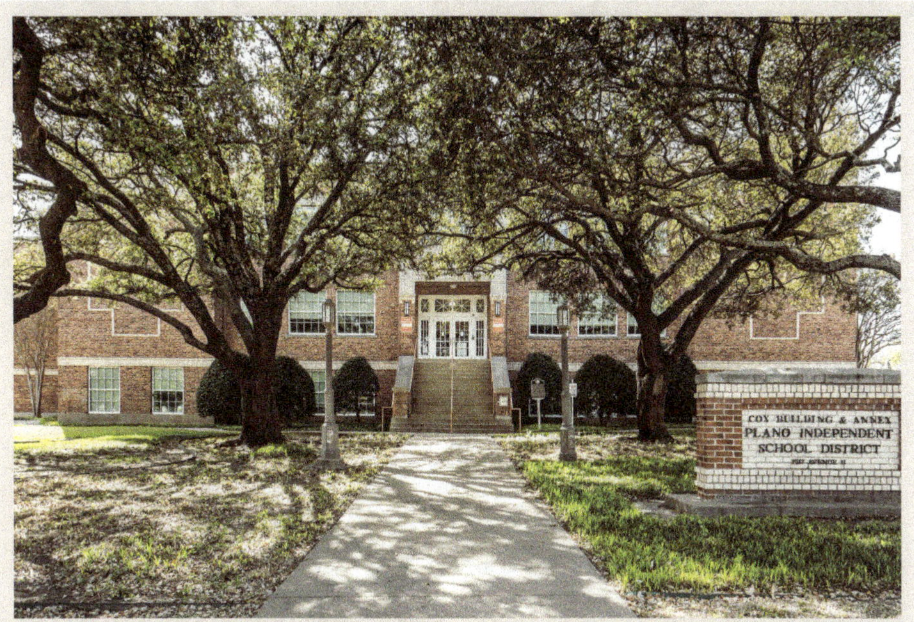


In 1903, the newly independent Plano schools opened a new three-story, redbrick building featuring a distinctive Spanish architectural style. In 1924, with enrollment growth, the "Old Spanish School" was replaced with a new building; it is now the Cox Building and home to PISD's administrative offices.

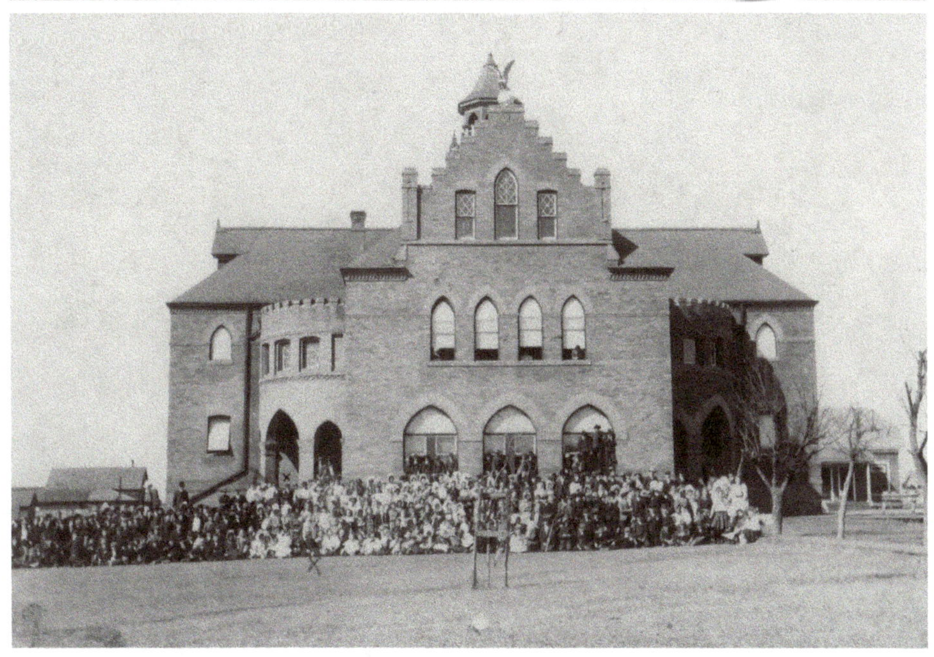

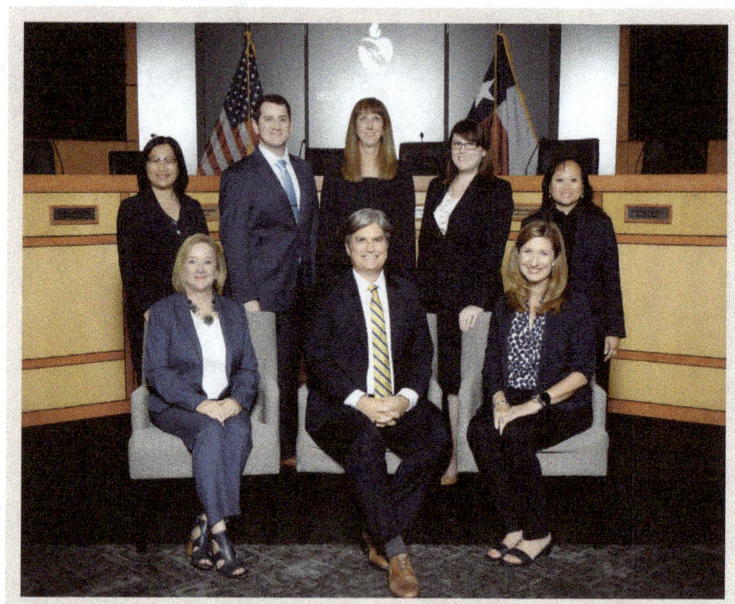

The vintage photograph below, taken around 1895–1898, shows the Plano school board and members of the faculty, including the superintendent and two music teachers. The 2021 photograph shows the PISD Board of Trustees who served 2021–2023, with then-superintendent Sara Bonser, standing in the center. (Present, courtesy of PISD.)

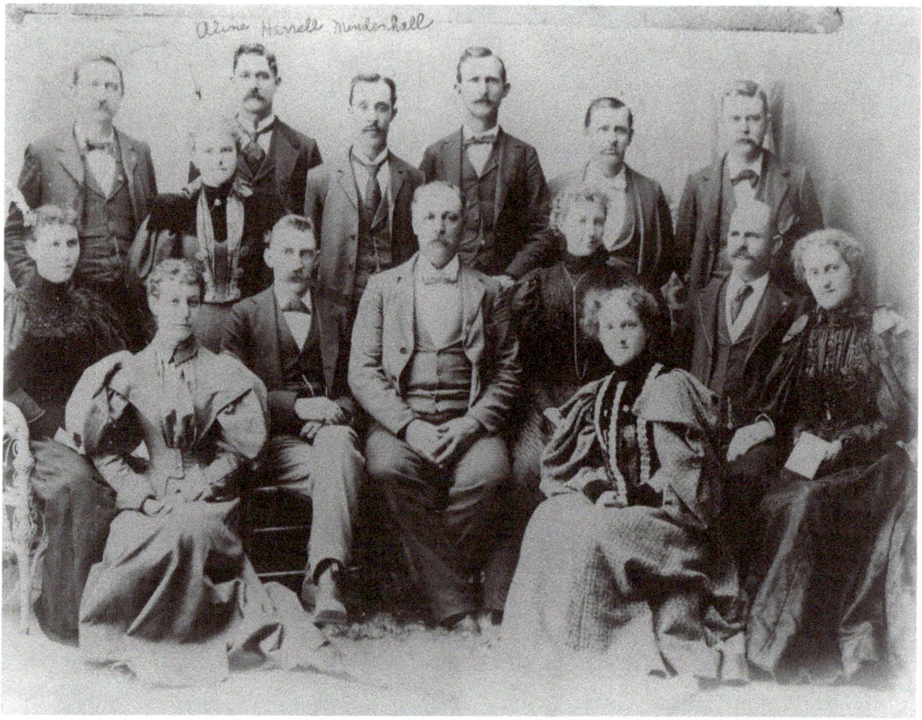

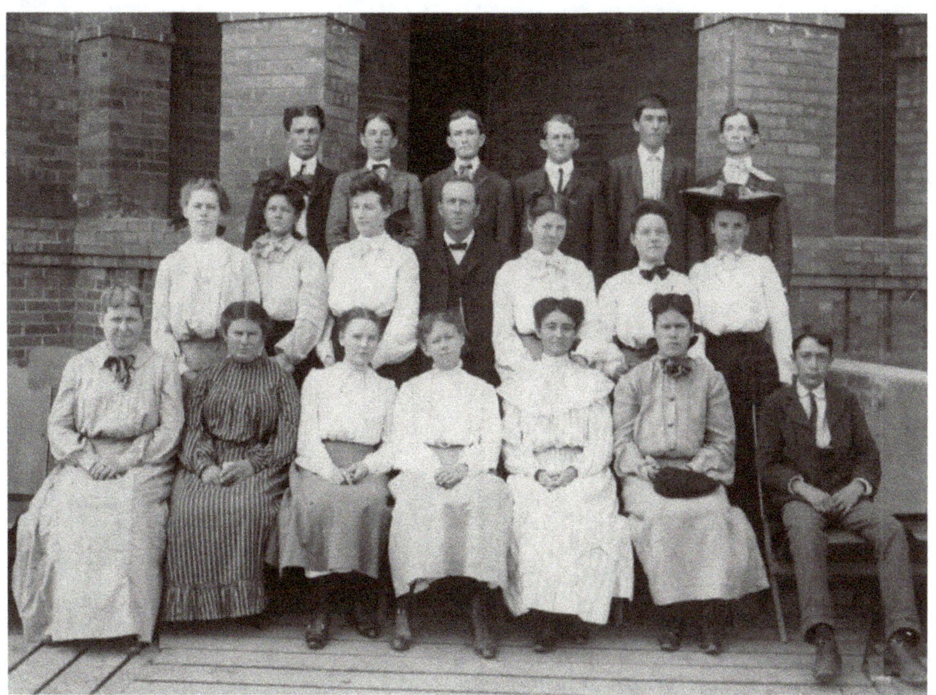

The Plano High School seniors of 1906 posed for a class photograph. Margaret Schimelpfenig Crawford later recalled that each graduate read an essay, either original or copied from Plato, Aristotle, or another philosopher, at commencement. Pictured in 2023 are members of the Plano Youth Leadership program, which equips students to "make well-informed life choices and to position themselves as leaders in their communities." The 36 Plano sophomore students were selected from area high schools. (Present, courtesy of Steve Lavine.)

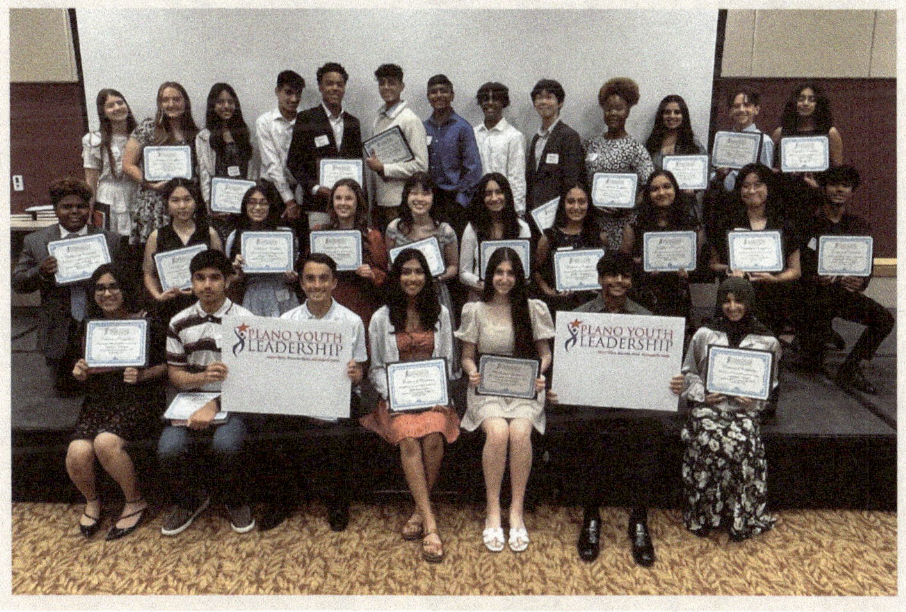

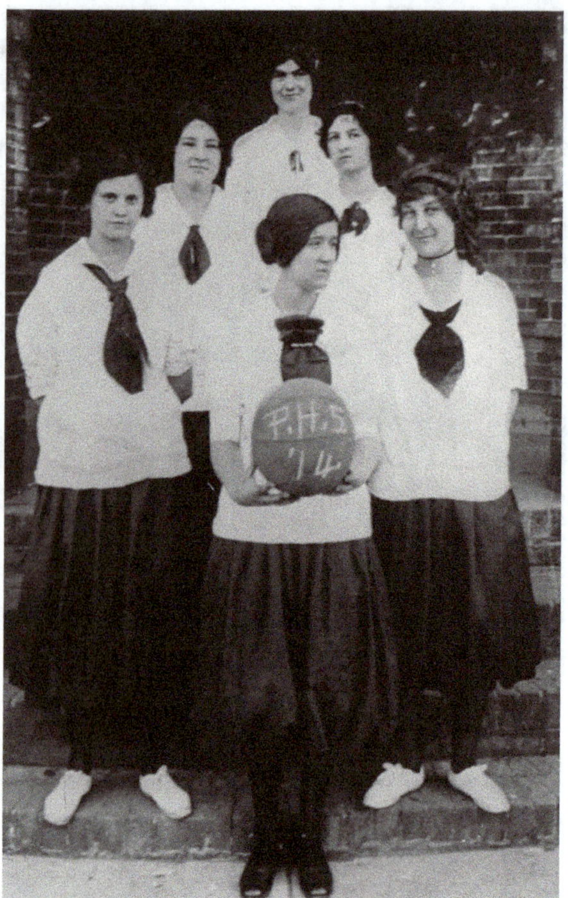


Pictured are members of the Plano girls' basketball team at Plano High School in 1914, coached by a Miss Higginbotham. In 2018, the Plano Senior High girls' basketball team captured its first state title ever. Plano Senior won the Class 6A girls' basketball championship with a 62-58 victory over Converse Judson at the Alamodome. The current photograph was taken in 2018. (Present, photograph by Kim Peichel.)

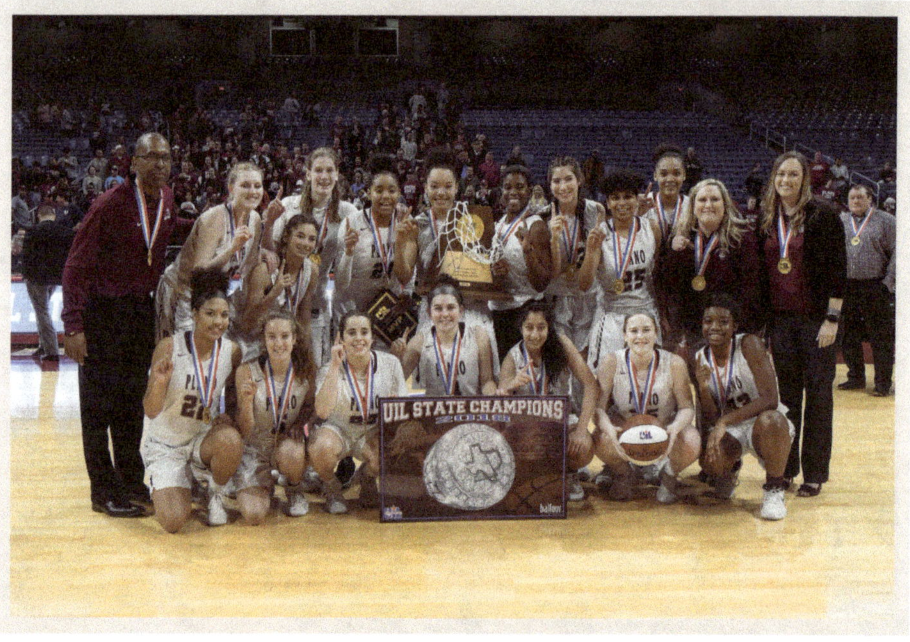

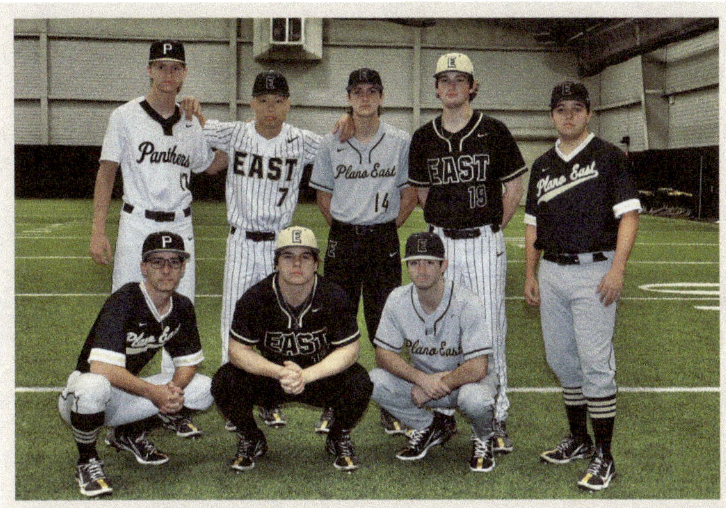


The vintage image shows members of the Plano High School baseball team in 1914. The two young boys are mascots Albert and Clint Blackman, sons of school superintendent A.M. Blackman (in black hat). Pictured above are class of 2023 seniors from Plano East Senior High's baseball team in a photograph taken in the Plano East fieldhouse. (Present, courtesy of Jennifer Bergman.)

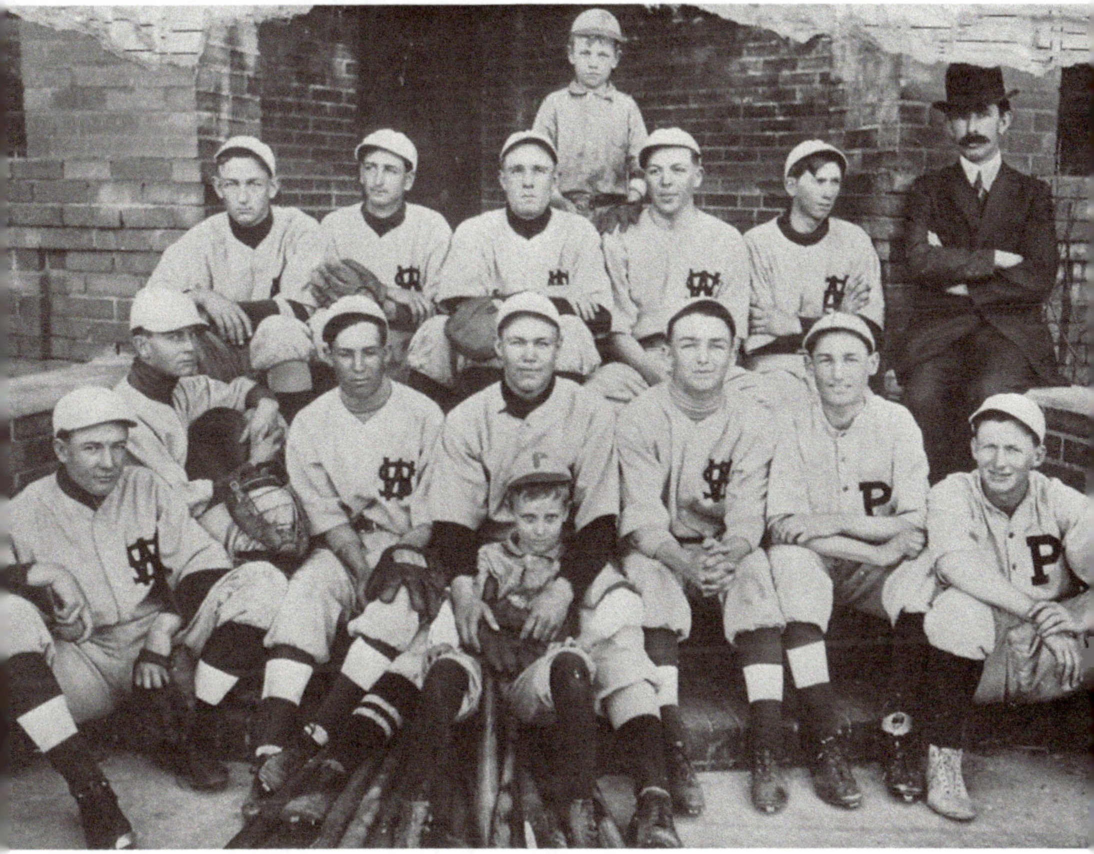

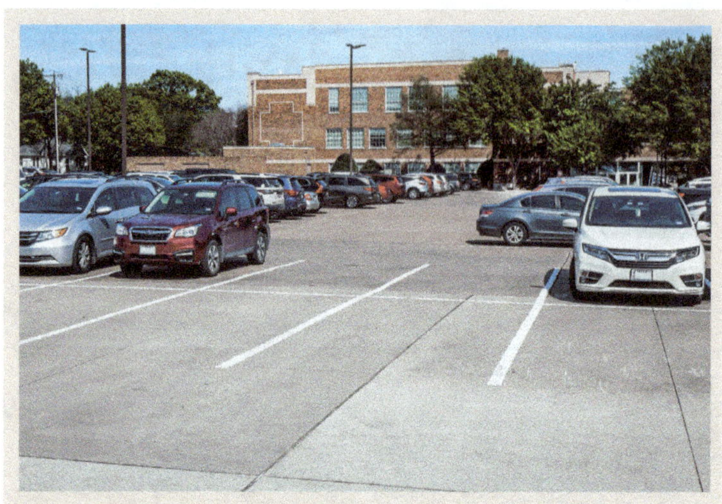

Members of the Plano Wildcats football team practice on the field behind the Cox Schoolhouse in a photograph from Plano High School's 1954 edition of the Planonian yearbook. The modern image shows the back of the same building, now known as the Cox Building, which today serves as the PISD's administration building.

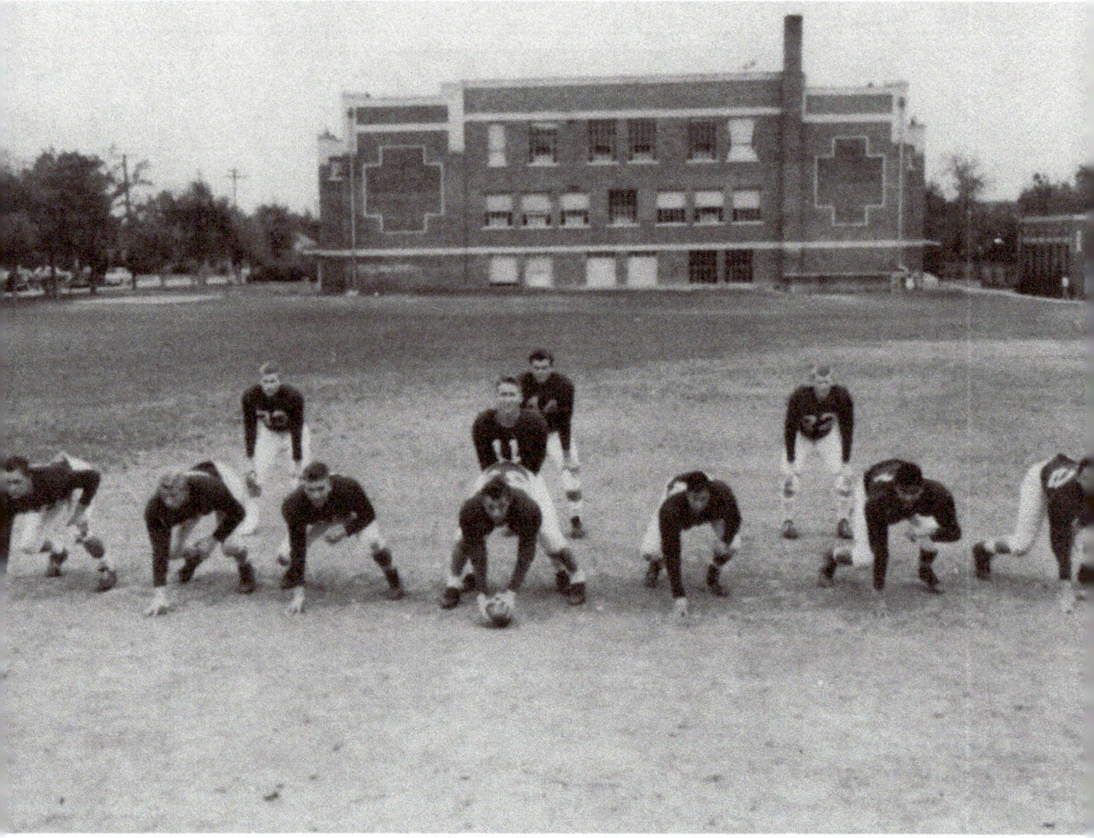

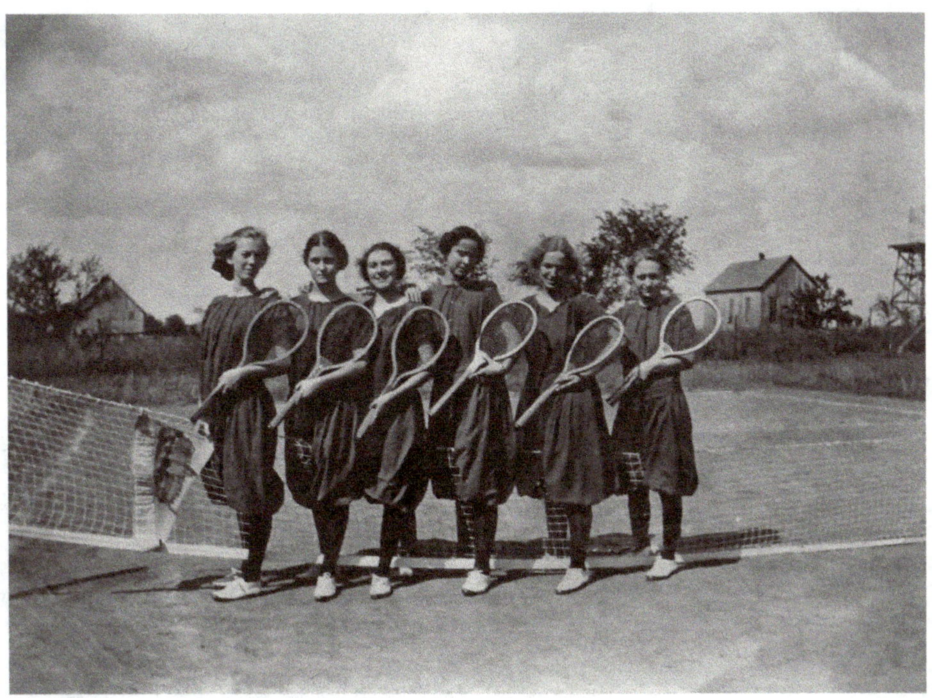

The vintage photograph shows a group of high school tennis players in the early 20th century in Plano (exact location unknown.) The 2023 image features high school players in the High Performance program at the City of Plano's High Point Tennis Center, part of the Parks and Recreation Department, located at 421 West Spring Creek Parkway. They are, from left to right, Dana Boteva, Maya Aguirre, Karla Brown, Eva Kovachev, Natalye Montemayor, and Medha Chandana.

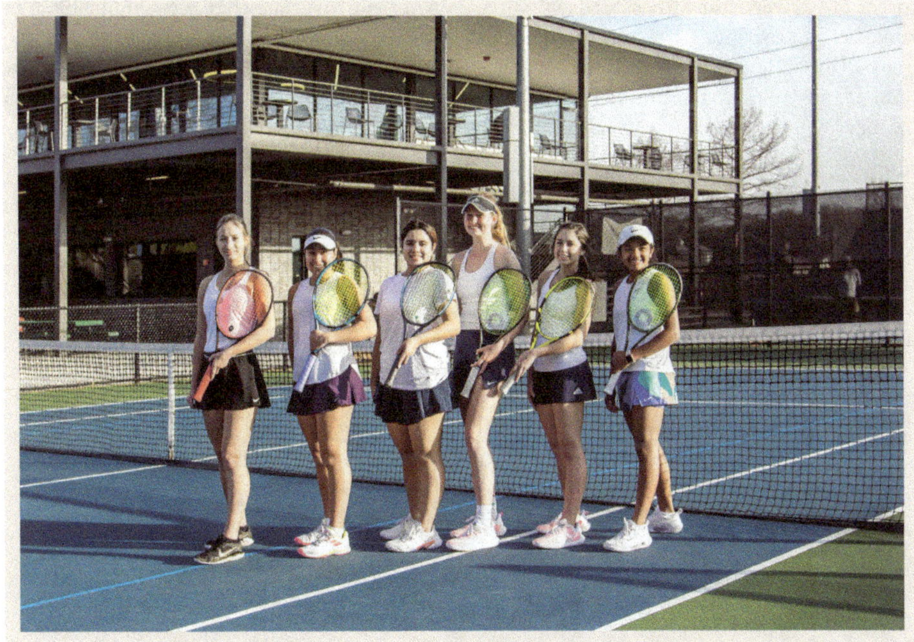

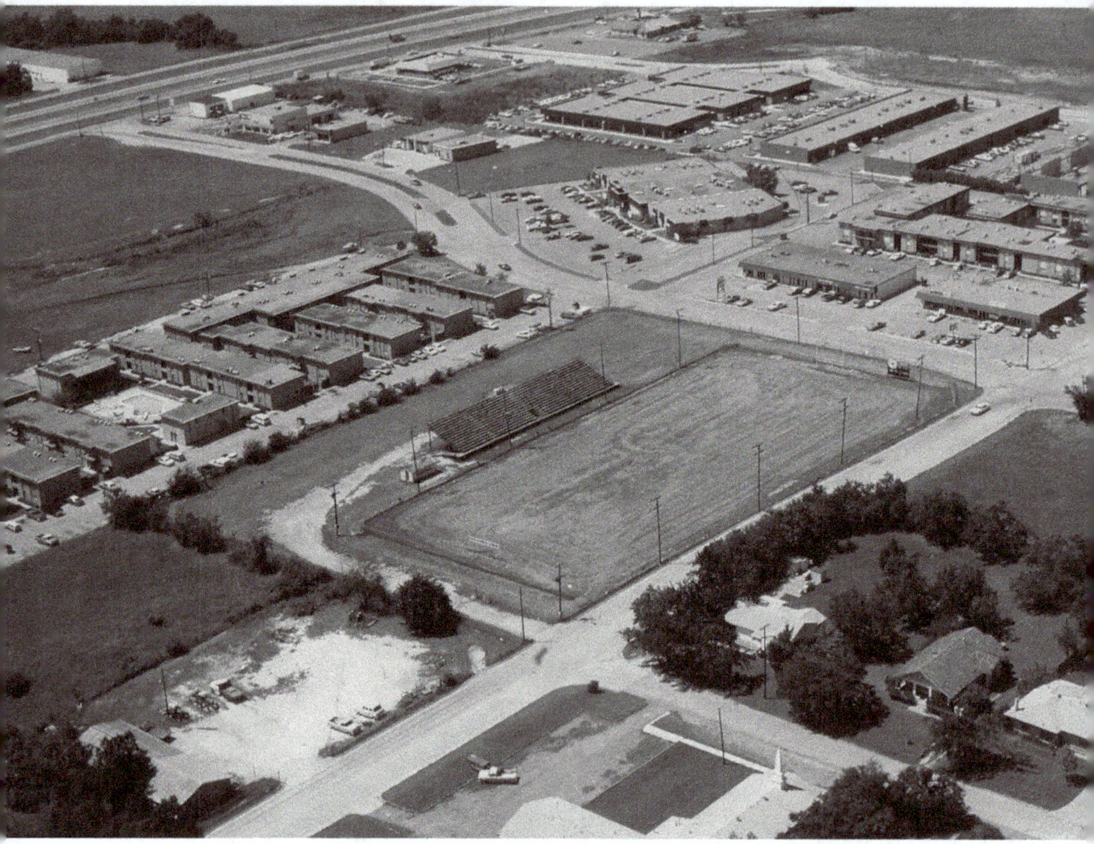

From 1925 to 1963, Rice Field (at the southwest corner of G Avenue and 18th Street) was the home field for two football teams: the Wildcats from Plano High School and the Panthers from Plano Colored High School. In 1964, the newly integrated Plano Wildcats moved into Wildcat Stadium (Williams Field) and won their first state championship in 1965. In 2018, the Rice Field area was redeveloped into a residential neighborhood. The aerial view was captured in 2023. (Present, photograph by Jason Lavine.)

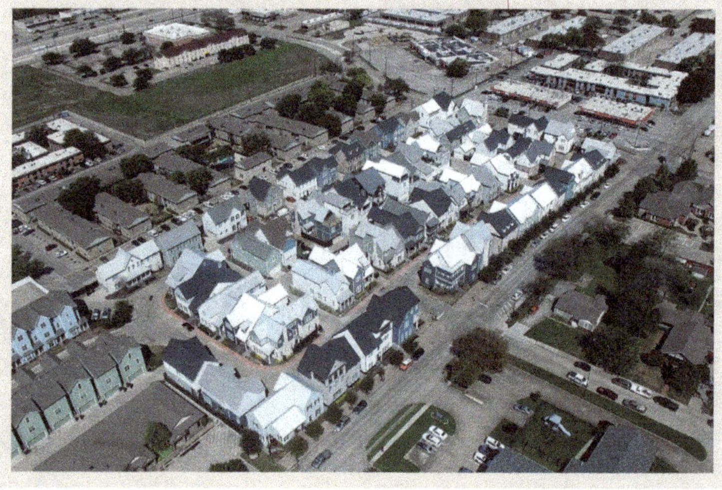

# About the Authors

Mary Jacobs is an award-winning freelance writer who writes regularly for the *Dallas Morning News*, the Silver Century, and other outlets. Mary was one of the founding organizers of TEDxPlano in 2014 and served as a speaker in 2017. Formerly a producer of Plano Podcast, Mary was named a *Plano Magazine* Girlboss in 2017. She is a member of the Board of the Plano Conservancy for Historic Preservation and received the Conservancy's Maggie Sprague Volunteer of the Year Award in 2021. The History Press published Mary's first book, *Haunted Plano, Texas*, in 2018. Mary is also coauthor of *Hidden History of Plano* (2020, The History Press) along with Jeff Campbell and Cheryl Smith.

Cheryl Smith is a public services librarian with the Plano Public Library. Through her library work as a genealogy research expert, she has helped make Collin County historical images and documents available for public viewing online and has transcribed many of the handwritten documents, diaries, and notes in the Plano Public Library collections, including those of the Plano Volunteer Fire Department and the Thursday Study Club.

Jeff Campbell is the director of the Plano Conservancy for Historic Preservation. He writes about Plano history for *Plano Magazine* and also coauthored *Football and Integration in Plano, Texas: Stay in There, Wildcats!* (The History Press, 2014), and *Plano's Historic Cemeteries* (Arcadia Publishing, 2014). Jeff has worked on historic preservation projects in Texas, Louisiana, and New Mexico. He serves on the board of the Texas Chapter of the Association of Gravestone Studies. Jeff is also the author of *Texas Bluegrass History* (The History Press, 2021).

Jennifer Shertzer is a freelance photographer and graphic designer who cofounded *Plano Magazine* in 2014 along with her husband, Luke. As editor, Jennifer curated content reflecting Plano's diverse and vibrant community. In 2021, Jennifer and Luke were honored with the Arts Impresario Award from the ArtCentre of Plano. In 2019, she won the Rising Star Award from the Plano Chamber of Commerce. She currently serves on the Leadership Plano advisory board. A graduate of Plano Citizens Academy, Jennifer is also the Public Image Chair for Plano West Rotary Club and sits on the Arts Advisory Board for North Texas Performing Arts.

www.ingramcontent.com/pod-product-compliance
Lightning Source LLC
LaVergne TN
LVHW010951100826
845153LV00002B/202

*9781540257574*